Prophet and Poet

PROPHET
and
POET

---

*The Bible
and the Growth of
Romanticism*

MURRAY ROSTON

NORTHWESTERN
UNIVERSITY PRESS
Evanston

To FAITH

in gratitude and affection

Contents

Abbreviations Used

EHR   *English Historical Review*
ELH   *Journal of English Literary History*
ES   *Essays and Studies*
JEGP   *Journal of English and Germanic Philology*
JHI   *Journal of the History of Ideas*
JR   *Journal of Religion*
JTS   *Journal of Theological Studies*
MLN   *Modern Language Notes*
MLR   *Modern Language Review*
MP   *Modern Philology*
PMLA   *Publications of the Modern Language Association of America*
PQ   *Philological Quarterly*
RES   *Review of English Studies*
SP   *Studies in Philology*

Preface

The recent revival of interest in early eighteenth-century poetry has placed the romantics in partial eclipse. But poetic fashions ought not to be regarded as mutually exclusive. If the school of Pope excelled in achieving a charming delicacy, a satirical urbanity in its verse, the romantics were afire with the splendours of the natural world and with a sense of the lofty function of poetry as a spiritual guide for mankind. This 'prophetic' quality is not, I believe, fortuitous. Those preromantic poets writing during the period of transition from Pope to Wordsworth had been searching, for the most part unconsciously, for some august literary model under whose aegis they could break away from those authoritative 'rules' for poetry derived from the classics. And in the rediscovery of biblical poetry they found one gateway to the new literary world. For if the Bible had long formed part of their cultural heritage, its imaginative and spiritual impact upon English verse had been severely limited by the obscurity of its poetic techniques. The realization that Isaiah did, in fact, write in poetry, and that his poetry was filled with passion, fire, and moral vision, gave to the preromantics that model for which they had been searching.

The debt of English romanticism to this new interest in biblical poetry, while it has been acknowledged, has never been closely studied, and it is the purpose of this book to examine in some detail the nature and extent of that debt, both in the narrower sphere of metrical forms and in those broader concepts of poetry peculiar to the romantic movement. Such an investigation inevitably involves even wider issues, and this book is really a study of Hebraism and Classicism against an eighteenth-century background.

Since we are concerned here with the specifically Hebraic influence of the Bible, the terms *Bible* and *biblical* are used

13

throughout with reference only to the Old Testament. Biblical quotations are from the Authorized Version except where that translation obscures or deviates from the Hebrew original, when I have emended accordingly. I follow Van Tieghem in employing the term *preromanticism* to indicate the period of transition between neo-classical and romantic poetry. It is as imprecise as all such literary categorizations, but it serves a useful function in denoting those trends towards more personal, emotional poetry distinguishable in eighteenth-century literature.

I should like to express my thanks to Professors David Daiches, J. Isaacs, and James Sutherland, who read the manuscript at various stages of completion in England, and to those American colleagues who were kind enough to read it in its more complete form while I was teaching at Brown University —Professors S. Foster Damon, Edward A. Bloom, and Charles Glicksberg. Finally, I owe a special debt of gratitude to Professor Harold Fisch of Bar-Ilan University, without whose initial suggestion and subsequent encouragement the book would never have been written.

I am also grateful to the Trustees of Bar-Ilan University for a generous research grant which facilitated the publication of this book.

Bar-Ilan University
Ramat Gan, Israel

1

Hebraism and Classicism

Hellenism and Hebraism, that strangely ill-assorted pair, produced in Western culture an offspring of their union, and it
has become a pastime of historians and critics to distinguish,
like fond aunts, the features of each parent in the child.

It is easy to oversimplify the distinction between them.
Heine, for example, looked for the ascetic, apocalyptic tradition of the Bible as though the Bible had abhorred the worldly
blessings of flocks, herds and vineyards. And to the Greek
world he attributed the vigorous realism of contemporary life
as though Plato had not dreamed of an impossibly idealistic
republic. Yet there was some validity in his generalization, and
Matthew Arnold's extension of it provides us with a useful
starting-point. For Arnold distinguished between the Hebraic
concern with right *acting* and the Hellenic insistence upon right
thinking; or, to put it differently, the almost exclusive concern
with moral probity in the Bible and the Greek delight in the
beauty and rationality of the idea.

The literatures of the two cultures have their roots firmly
embedded in their different soils. Hebrew literature, however
artistically splendid it may be, never ceases to be primarily
didactic in its intent, an instrument for impressing upon man
the enormity of his task in a moral universe; while for the
Greek, artistic perfection was a noble and worthy end in itself.
As Corydon and Thyrsis sing of their loves beneath the shady
tree of the classical pastoral, a third shepherd stretches
languorously beside them waiting to adjudicate the prize. For
all their protestations of undying devotion, the pastoral is
primarily a literary competition in which the prize is awarded

not for the fervour of the shepherd's passion, but for the artistry whereby he transmutes it into poetry. The nearest biblical counterparts to this pastoral scene are Nathan's allegory of the poor man's lamb and Ezekiel's denunciation of the wicked shepherds of Israel. In each, a grave moral preoccupation transforms the scene from an idyll into an image of a purposive world in which man must struggle eternally against sin and corruption.

The Greek poet began with an intellectual conception of beauty as the ideal towards which he must strive, polishing and improving his verse until it approached as near as was humanly possible to this ideal. His interest in literary criticism—from the analytical triumph of Aristotle's *Poetics* to the comic weighing of Euripides against Aeschylus in the *Frogs*—was symptomatic of the importance attached to literary aesthetics. The Dionysiac festival itself, for all its residue of primitive religious rites and its Aeschylean gropings towards monotheism, again took the form of a literary competition. Plato, so far from regarding literature as a moral weapon, tore up his own poetic drama when he turned to ethical problems and, with the reluctance of a naturally gifted poet, outlawed poetry from his republic as incompatible with morality and truth. The Roman poet, equally concerned with literature as an art, modelled himself closely on his Greek predecessor and wrote poems on the art of poetry. Verse became primarily a social act, to be performed with wit, urbanity, and (even in the caustic satires of Juvenal) with due regard for the conventions of literary form.

In contrast, the prophetic poetry of the Bible was fired with the urgency of the divine message, to which all verbal dexterity was subordinated. There lay behind all biblical verse a personal awareness of the Creator before whose wrath or love there was no room for witty antithesis or calculated tessellation. Antithesis there could be, but only to drive home a point, to emphasize a contrast, to impress an audience with a consciousness of its moral duties, but never to evoke applause for its wit. Biblical Hebrew has no word for *literature* and only the crudest terminology for distinguishing between literary genres.

16

For literature had a function to perform; and the fact that a psalm of praise was also a literary masterpiece, that the story of Ruth was a triumph of prose, and the book of Isaiah a poetic as well as a divine vision, was regarded as a valuable side-product rather than an ultimate ideal. Ezekiel wrote scornfully of 'the love song of one that hath a pleasant voice and can play well on an instrument' as an image of valueless entertainment. Right acting, the ability to distinguish between good and evil and to choose the good, that was man's primary duty in the world, and the Greek's striving after artistic perfection as an end in itself was totally foreign to the biblical poet.

For the biblical poet, the moral connotations with which the pastoral scene was replete were deepened by the knowledge that the sheep, like man himself, formed part of a divine creation. The stories of the patriarchs and kings are more than historical narrative and, as Erich Auerbach has shown, differ greatly from the Homeric epic.[1] Where the latter describes the courage, virtue, and loves of 'heroes' or demigods, the Old Testament account is concerned only with men, fallible men, struggling against their own weaknesses to achieve some degree of righteousness. Yet even these are not particularized accounts restricted to specific historical characters, but by their elemental simplicity suggest some universal significance valid for all generations. Nowhere does the Bible define the ultimate purpose of creation, nor more than allude in the most oblique terms to man's function on earth. But behind the pageant of biblical narrative hangs the enormous backcloth which gives meaning, coherence, and depth to the individual scenes—the backcloth of absolute moral values, of the paradox of man's insignificance yet dignity in the presence of God, of the immanence of the Creator in the grandeur of Nature itself.

This contrast between classical and biblical literature was never so apparent as in the eighteenth century. In every generation from St. Jerome onward, the Christian had felt the pull away from the Bible and toward the literary brilliance of the classics. But this was partly because he had only a remote

[1] Erich Auerbach, *Mimesis* (New York, 1957), p. 5.

17

idea of the specific nature of biblical literature. The distinction between prose and verse in the Hebrew original had been forgotten during the generation which saw the rise of Christianity, and it was only in the eighteenth century that the theory of Hebrew poetry was rediscovered. Moreover, the period of its rediscovery coincided with an intense literary identification with the Augustan age of Rome—an identification which permeated the philosophy, the sensibility, and the moral fibre of the age. Horace had become the model not only for poetry but also for the neo-classical urbanity, restraint, and sophisticated detachment from life. Neo-classicism never, of course, became an exact replica of its Roman model, but at least it made a conscious effort to capture that urbane detachment in its own writings, and the *Spectator* typified even in its name the ideal of the new scientific age to avoid personal involvement and to stand, as it were, at the sidelines, watching the hurly-burly of life with the curious amusement of a superior being.

The Bible, with its emotional intensity and its stern demand for moral integrity, was the very antithesis of such detachment, and our purpose here is to suggest how the rediscovery of the Bible as literature rather than as religious text helped to wean the eighteenth-century poet away from his classical model and to mould not merely his poetic techniques but also his literary sensibility. I should like at this point to disclaim any intention of suggesting that this antithesis was the prime, or even a primary cause of romanticism. Professor Lovejoy warned us long ago of the dangers inherent in the very term 'romanticism' which covers an entire complex of literary and aesthetic trends; and there can be little doubt that, whatever currents and cross-currents swirled below the surface, the tide was bound to turn against Reason before long. I do propose to argue, however, that an awareness of this eighteenth-century clash between Classicism and Hebraism can provide a richer understanding of the growth and development of both preromantic and romantic poetry which, in their trend towards more vivid, emotional verse, found in the imaginative ethos and in the literary forms of the Old Testament a model ideally suited to their needs.

18

(I)

The indifference to literary form as such in the Scriptures was reflected in the very mechanics of its poetry. For Hebrew verse is so loosely constructed and so free from metrical rigidity that, during the two-thousand-year period when its techniques had been forgotten, neither Jewish nor Christian scholars were able to distinguish between the prose and verse sections of the Bible. All admitted that certain passages were poetic in their imagery and emotional resonance but, since in the original Hebrew manuscripts such passages were with rare exceptions set out continuously as prose, it was difficult to determine the line of demarcation between poetry and poetic prose. Even in the English translation the poetic quality of such passages was evident, for the imagery and rhythms were anything but prosaic:

Hear my prayer, O Lord, and let my cry come unto thee. Hide not thy face from me in the day when I am in trouble; incline thine ear unto me; in the day when I call, answer me speedily. For my days are consumed like smoke, and my bones are burned as an hearth. My heart is smitten, and withered like grass; so that I forget to eat my bread.

In the past, before 'free verse' was known and after the alliterative parallelistic verse of the Middle Ages had been forgotten, people thought of poetry as writing bound, to some extent at least, by a quantitative or accentual metre, but the poetical sections of the Bible refused to conform to any system upon which scholars could agree. Moreover, conflicting views on the correct pronunciation of Hebrew served both to hamper the investigator of metre and to encourage a harvest of fanciful theories. A comparison of an unrhymed passage from one of T. S. Eliot's poems written out as prose with part of a sermon by Donne would, perhaps, best illustrate the problem confronting the biblical scholar in his attempt to identify the poetry of the Bible. The firm rhythmic pattern and the vivid imagery indicated that it was poetry, but the absence of a regular metre suggested prose.

The traditional evidence on which such a scholar could rely

was both vague and contradictory. Philo, in his role as the interpreter of Judaism attempting to find parallels between Hebraic and Hellenic culture, had employed the term *hexameter* somewhat loosely to describe the standard Hebraic line. This term may have proved a useful means of conveying some inkling of biblical poetry to the non-Hebraist, but it was dangerously misleading to subsequent scholars once the techniques of that verse had been lost. For it suggested that Hebrew poetry could be scanned according to the exacting requirements of the classical metrical system, either quantitatively or (later) accentually. And Philo's statement carried particular weight with later generations as his is the last recorded statement by one who still understood how biblical poetry was composed. In the works of Josephus, who had inherited Philo's role as the interpreter of Judaism to the classical world and was therefore similarly concerned with employing classical terminology, the Psalms were described as composed of trimeters and pentameters, and this attempt to establish parallels with the classics succeeded merely in confusing the leaders of the Church. Jerome spoke of quasi-sapphics and heroics, admitting with some perplexity that certain passages appeared to be composed in poetry free from metre.[1]

The Jews themselves offered little guidance, and, in fact, were uninterested in the literary dispute. The primary concerns of such commentators as Rashi and Kimchi were elucidation of the text and homiletical exegesis. Literary evaluation lay outside their province. When the medieval poet Judah Halevi arose within their midst, he turned to Arabic poetry for his metres, creating a new type of Hebrew verse dependent on the Bible only for its vocabulary and idiom.

By the seventeenth century, Christian belief in the quantitative interpretation had been shaken and scholars were divided. Some like George Wither rejected all attempts to scan

---

[1] Philo, *De Vita Contemplativa*, quoted in I. Baroway, 'Hebrew Hexameter', *ELH*, ii (1935). Baroway discusses this further in his 'Accentual Theory of Hebrew Prosody', *ELH*, xvii (1950). See also Josephus, *Antiquities*, vii, xii, and Jerome, *Epistola ad Paulum*.

biblical passages according to classical metre, while such determined metrists as Franciscus Gomarus went to the absurd lengths of distinguishing in one chapter of Job a complex metre involving antispastics, paeonics, choriambics and other rarely used scansional feet.[1] One wonders what he would have made of the Highway Code.

The solution to the problem came from an unexpected source. The appointment of Robert Lowth in 1741 to the professorship of Poetry at Oxford seemed totally unconnected with the problems of Hebrew versification. He was elected because of his wide reputation for classical learning and the elegance of his own Latin poems, and scholars assumed that, like the previous occupants of the chair, he would either regard his appointment as a sinecure or devote himself to general literary criticism as Joseph Trapp had done in his *Lectures on Poetry*. Surprisingly, however, Lowth combined his literary and ecclesiastical scholarship to deliver during the ten years of his occupancy some thirty-four lectures on *The Sacred Poetry of the Hebrews*. Although Lowth is today almost unknown outside the realm of biblical scholarship, in his own day his lectures were acclaimed as a milestone of general literary criticism which happened to use the Bible as its subject-matter. In fact, as only the more perceptive of his contemporaries realized, the reverse was true. For the new literary standards which he enunciated were evolved from the Bible itself, from his readiness to lay aside the literary assumptions of his age and to approach the Bible without preconceived notions. And the starting point of his work was the metrical theory for which he coined the name 'parallelism'.[2]

The first pointer to the new theory he found in the frequent references to antiphonal singing, which was probably an

---

[1] G. Wither, *A Preparation to the Psalter* (1619) (London, 1884), p. 59. For a discussion of Gomarus see I. Baroway, 'The Lyre of David', *ELH*, viii (1941).

[2] Details of previous occupants of the Chair can be found in G. Saintsbury, *A History of Criticism* (Edinburgh/London, 1917), iii, 615–16. Lowth's lectures, published in their original Latin in 1753, were translated into English by G. Gregory as *The Sacred Poetry of the Hebrews* in 1787. Quotations are from the London edition of 1835.

ancient tradition before the first books of the Bible were written. Miriam, taking a timbrel on the shore of the Red Sea,
answered Moses in words similar in sense and rhythm to his
own; and when David returned from slaughtering the Philistines, the women '. . . *answered* one another as they played and
said, Saul hath slain his thousands, and David his ten thousands'. This last verse suggests two groups of women singers,
one of which sang the first half of the verse *Saul hath slain his
thousands* while the second responded with *and David his ten
thousands*. Whether or not this particular passage was rendered antiphonally is immaterial. It is clear, however, that an
early antiphonal tradition had moulded the form of Hebrew
poetry not merely by dividing the line into two halves, but by
ensuring that the second section should echo (by corroboration
or contrast) the meaning of the first. The effect of such parallelism is to establish in Hebrew poetry a rhythmic ebb and flow,
a sense which doubles back upon itself, rather than the linear
forward movement of classical verse. But even more important
it employs instead of the rigid metrical laws of Greece and
Rome a loose structural relationship of phrases, parisonic only
insofar as each verse could be sung to the same tune.

If one sets out a biblical passage line by line, the parallelism
can be seen more clearly.

> When Israel went out of Egypt,
>   The house of Jacob from a strange people,
> Judah was his sanctuary,
>   Israel his dominion.
> The sea saw and fled,
>   The Jordan turned back,
> The mountains skipped like rams,
>   The hills like children of the flock.

One may well ask how Philo, who was one of the last writers
acquainted with the forms of Hebrew verse, could describe so
loose a structure as a 'hexameter', and the reason is very likely
the following. Where the classical metre contained six clearly
defined feet, Hebrew verse was usually composed of six verbal
'units', the last three of which reflected, amplified, or modified
the meaning of the first half-verse. In the passage set out

above, the first line contains in the Hebrew three verbal units

When-went-out/Israel/from-Egypt

answered by a further three units

The-house-of-Jacob/from-a-people/strange.

Such verse is not to be scanned syllabically but according to its firm sense-rhythm supported by an approximate verbal rhythm, the meaning of the verse always dominating its texture.

The analysis of Hebrew poetry can be carried into many further categories and sub-divisions, but the main point is already clear. In Hebrew verse, artistic form is subordinated to the subject-matter, and it is the sense of the passage itself which creates the rhythm. Where a Latin poem is invalidated by even one false syllable, Hebrew verse employs a flexible, undulatory rhythm produced neither by syllabic quantity nor by accentuation, but by the antiphonal sense-pattern of the passage. And perhaps even more important is the self-generating emotional force of parallelism, which pulsates in rhythmic unison with the sense.

The distinction between the balance of phrases in parallelism and the apparently similar balance of the neo-classical heroic couplet is subtle, but nonetheless profound. Pope's verse exploits the firm metrical framework to create a brilliant series of contrasts and juxtapositions. The pauses dictated by the metre leave the key words echoing in the mind and allow the reader to savour the witty ambivalences.

> On her white breast a sparkling Cross she wore,
> Which Jews might kiss, and Infidels adore.

We pause at *breast* with its erotic associations. The main accent is next thrown on *Cross*, so that in the following line *kiss* and *adore*, while ostensibly directed at *Cross*, are, of course, really intended for the young lady's bosom. And as we grasp the *double entendre*, at another level we are responding to the pun on the physical and religious meanings of *adore*. In biblical parallelism, however, there is no framework other than the pulsating sense, and the effect is to suggest that the poet has

23

returned to the phrase through sheer joy or sorrow in the statement itself.

> The sea saw and fled,
> The Jordan turned back.

Where Pope deliberately gives the impression of playing a game (sometimes the very serious game of ridiculing the absurd), biblical parallelism both reflects and creates an emotional impulse essentially closer to romantic than to neo-classical poetry:

> No motion has she now, no force:
> She neither hears nor sees.

The simplicity of biblical style, so frequently praised from Longinus onwards, owes its source largely to this parallelist form; for the separation into independent hemistychs demands a basic simplicity of structure. Since each half-verse represents a unit of sense-rhythm, its meaning must be self-contained, and hence complexity of sentence structure is automatically precluded. A glance at the previous biblical quotation will confirm that each half-verse, if not a complete sentence, is at least a complete idea—a technique which encouraged the simple juxtaposition of ideas rather than subordination. Those participial phrases, involved subordinate clauses and climactic periods so beloved by the classics have no counterpart in the Bible, which prefers to achieve its rhetorical effects by abrupt, concise sentences joined by a single conjunction. 'And I will cut thee off from the people, and I will cause thee to perish out of the countries: I will destroy thee; and thou shalt know that I am the Lord.'

But perhaps the most significant difference resulting from this parallelist simplicity is the concrete suggestiveness of biblical imagery, which rarely alludes adjectivally but draws, as it were, a tangible simile. With only the few words of a hemistych to express an idea, the poet must reduce his image to a vividly concise picture and compensate for the lack of detail by the sharpness of the comparison. Where Homer and Vergil delight in the extended image which serves to embellish the narrative, the biblical poet cannot allow himself any

24

leisurely digression from the urgent subject-matter, and the resultant effect is a more brilliantly focused imagery than that of classical and neo-classical literature. For all his worship of 'perspicuity' the Augustan poet would write somewhat vaguely of his love:

> O ruddier than the Cherry
> O sweeter than the Berry,
> O nymph more bright
> Than Moonshine Night. . . .

The Hebrew, however, conveys concretely the sense of touch, taste, or smell on which the comparison is based:

Thy stature is like to a palm tree and thy breasts to clusters of grapes. I said, I will go up to the palm tree, I will take hold of the boughs thereof: now also shall thy breasts be as the clusters of the vine and the smell of thy nose like apples.[1]

By the second verse the maiden's figure has merged with the palm tree to become one with it. It is the absence of this particularization and tangibility which leaves us wondering in the first passage whether the lady's sweetness is one of character, appearance, or even taste, and hence the poem presents us with a conventional and generalized picture. It may, perhaps, be putting the cart before the horse to suggest that parallelism encouraged this concreteness of imagery and simplicity of diction; for if Hebrew sensibility had inclined to the discursive rather than the vividly particular it would, no doubt, have moulded parallelism to its own taste. But at least we may recognize that parallelism as it developed in the Bible is admirably suited to such particularization.

The tangibility of biblical metaphor is profoundly reinforced by the peculiar linguistic development of Hebrew. For all Hebrew words grew out of simple triliteral roots and, even in their most complex forms, retain the elemental force of these roots. It is impossible to translate the phrase 'As a mother has mercy upon her children' without losing almost all the effect; for the Hebrew word *to have mercy* is a derivative of the word for *womb*. Of course all translation loses some of the subtlety

---

[1] John Gay, *Acis and Galatea* and *Cant.*, vii, 7.

and ambivalence of its original, but where these ambivalences are in most languages comparatively rare, the linguistic development of Hebrew ensured that almost every word preserved the mark of its ancestry and hence much of its original simplicity. Even the word for a *sword*, itself a comparatively simple noun, is a derivative of the triliteral root *to dry up*, and thus carries connotations evocative of the natural rather than the civilized world. Warfare becomes a form of blight which ruins the harvest and prevents each man from sitting peacefully beneath his luxuriant vine; and the beating of swords into ploughshares has deeper associations than can possibly be conveyed in translation.

The corollary is that no matter how far Hebraic civilization might advance, it could never lose contact with the primitive natural world out of which it had sprung. Classical literature (and neo-classical even more so) tended to artificialize the natural world in the process of transforming it into poetry. A gulf existed between the stylized pastoral and the real world of mud and manure, and it was a gulf which Hebrew poetry could neither create nor tolerate, for no vocabulary existed which was free of these everyday associations. The Bible did not 'elevate' prosaic diction to a poetic sphere but used all its daily connotations to reinforce the poetic content. Such ambivalences as were deliberately cultivated were far nearer metaphysical usage than neo-classical. Hosea's brilliant image of Israel as the fallen woman contains God's offer of reconciliation 'I shall betroth thee to me in faith, and thou shalt *know* the Lord'. The word *know* carries with it undertones of marital union, in the physical sense that Adam *knew* his wife and she conceived. Such word-play in a profoundly serious passage serves to underscore the binding marital force of the covenant. On the other hand, the epitaph to the architect Vanbrugh

> Lie heavy on him, Earth! for he
> Laid many heavy loads on thee![1]

[1] Abel Evans, *On Sir John Vanbrugh*. H. Fisch offers a penetrating examination of biblical ambivalence in 'The Analogy of Nature', *JTS*, vi (1955).

(all differences in subject-matter apart) illustrates the neo-classicist's greater delight in verbal dexterity for its own sake.

Moreover, the Hebrew poet, intoxicated by the splendour and power of his Creator, turns all attention from himself, a mere mortal or *son of man*, towards his subject-matter: he gains his effect by something approaching what T. S. Eliot called the 'process of depersonalisation', by transmuting passions without obtruding his own personality upon them. Once more, he is concerned primarily with the spirit, with the divine message, and he is almost unconscious of himself in the role of the poet. When the poet of the eighteenth century describes the sinking of a ship, he reveals little of his own emotion however deeply moved he may be, but, by commenting upon the scene, by standing, as it were, between the reader and the event, he produces a controlled, restrained elegy with conscious declamatory effect.

> Toll for the Brave—
>   The Brave! that are no more:
> All sunk beneath the wave,
>   Fast by their native shore.
> Eight hundred of the Brave,
>   Whose courage well was tried,
> Had made the vessel heel
>   And laid her on her side.

In contrast, the biblical poet is afire with the excitement of the scene, now identifying himself with the enemy and savouring their false confidence, now triumphing in God's supreme power.

The enemy said, I will pursue, I will overtake. I will divide the spoil, my soul shall be satisfied on them. I will draw my sword, my hand shall destroy them. Thou didst blow with Thy wind, the sea covered them. They sank like lead in the mighty waters. Who is like Thee, O Lord![1]

The differences between classical and Hebrew poetry are examined below in more detail and, particularly, the elements in biblical poetry which could appeal to the early preromantics; but above all it was this passion and fire, this sense of

[1] Cowper, *On the Loss of the Royal George* and Exodus, xv, 9.

27

personal involvement and the ability to find God (and hence poetry) in the world of individual experience which distinguished Hebrew poetry from the poetry of Pope and his contemporaries.

(II)

That sense of humility before the Supreme Creator which pervades all biblical poetry contrasts vividly with the graceful self-assurance of the eighteenth-century poet. The prophet wrote of the glories of the messianic age, of sin and righteousness and, indeed, of subjects momentous in their import, before which he, the poet, was as nothing. But the Augustan poet, taking as his watchword the Horatian maxim that poetry must either amuse or instruct, was concerned primarily with the sparkling witticisms of the mock epic or the sententious didacticism of social satire. If the biblical poet prostrated himself in the dust before his Creator, the neo-classicist, conscious of the dignity befitting a rational creature, decked himself in the poetic finery of elevated diction and neatly balanced phrases. Perhaps, like the biblical poet, we should be more concrete and compare two passages similar in subject-matter but typical of the respective cultures.

For the Psalmist, even the orderliness of the tides, the bounds set for the oceans, formed subject-matter for an ecstatic song of praise, and the simplicity of diction reflects his wonder:

The waters stood above the mountains. At thy rebuke they fled; at the voice of thy thunder they hasted away. They go up by the mountains; they go down by the valleys unto the place which thou has founded for them. Thou hast set a bound that they may not pass over; that they turn not again to cover the earth.

The swift excitement of the passage is achieved largely by the concreteness of every word. Each noun is specific and exact; even the *rebuke* is the audible reprimand of the thunder, and the seas themselves are described in the elemental term *the waters*. All nature joins in the paean, trembling before the might of God, and this animistic effect is gained by the colourful verbs *stood, fled, hasted away,* and their human associations.

Matthew Prior's treatment of the identical theme provides an almost clinical specimen of the essential differences between the Hebraic and the neo-classical poetic techniques. Prior writes:

> Why should its num'rous Waters stay
> In comely Discipline, and fair Array,
> 'Till Winds and Tides exert their High Commands?
> Then prompt and ready to obey,
> Why do the rising Surges spread
> Their op'ning Ranks o'er Earth's submissive Head,
> Marching thro' different Paths to different Lands?[1]

The stanza produces a predominantly rhetorical effect, largely by means of the dramatic, unanswerable questions; and the primary emphasis is not, like the Psalmist's, on the enormous, latent powers of nature but on the *Discipline* whereby the waters *march* like orderly troops along their assigned paths. This, indeed, is merely a reflection of that detachment typical of the age, the restraint to prevent involvement, but it is the extension of this restraint into the smallest details of poetic technique which proves most illuminating. For in an attempt to avoid the sharpness of vivid portrayal, every noun and verb is deliberately blunted by the substitution of a circumlocutory phrase. The waters become the *rising Surges*; they do not *flee* but *spread their op'ning Ranks*; and where the biblical God *rebukes*, Prior's tides *exert their High Commands*.

This periphrastic device, however admirably it suited the needs of the age, was not entirely original nor yet mere plagiarism, but an intriguing combination of the two. It was classical in source, but I would suggest that it arose from the later student's attempt to master Latin rather than from Latin poetry itself. Of the forty-three poets included in Johnson's collection, whose lives fell either wholly or partly in the eighteenth century, all but one had a thorough grounding in classics either at school or university, and an integral part of

---

[1] Prior, *An Ode Written in 1688*, published in Dryden's *Miscellany* (1693).

that classical education was an intense training in Latin versification, in the translation, that is, of English verses into Latin hexameters and elegiacs. Indeed, most schoolboys studied English poetry through the spectacles of Latin verse and were introduced to the former only after they had been thoroughly '. . . lashed into Latin by the tingling rod'. Hoole insisted that pupils must be taught to scan Latin verse as a prerequisite for poetizing in English, and there is ample evidence that the same demands were made of the following generation of schoolboys.[1] Any similarities, therefore, between the devices which they were taught to employ in Latin versification and those employed in English verse are by no means fortuitous.

The quantitative character of Latin verse, in which a short vowel becomes lengthened when followed by two consonants, demanded from the versifier a veritable exercise in mental gymnastics, and what came more naturally to the Roman poet was for the schoolboy a sort of jigsaw puzzle requiring a vast vocabulary and considerable ingenuity. Mercifully, he was provided with a helpful thesaurus of words and phrases, the *Gradus ad Parnassum*. This grouped under each common noun a host of periphrases which themselves filled a substantial portion of the line.

In place of *death*, the schoolboy was encouraged to use the poetic elaboration *perpetual night* or *the dark day* which not only were sanctioned by classical usage but formed conveniently a prefabricated metrical unit. Under *piscis*, amid eight lines of periphrases, is included the familiar *gens squamigera* echoed in Pope's

With looks unmoved he hopes the *scaly breed*.

Isaiah knows no such 'scaly breeds' and with blunt clarity describes a divinely ordained drought in the terms 'Their fish stinketh because there is no water, and dieth of thirst.' But

[1] For details of this training see J. Sutherland, *Preface to Eighteenth Century Poetry* (Oxford, 1950), p. 50, and C. Hoole, *A New Discovery of the Old Art of Teaching Schoole* (London, 1660). Vicesimus Knox, *A Liberal Education* (London, 1781), shows that Latin versification continued to occupy a major place in eighteenth-century education too.

for Pope the device helped to raise poetry above the level of the mundane and indecorous. The place of the *Gradus* in moulding the style of neo-classical verse has been almost ignored by critics. Tillotson explains Pope's use of 'scaly breed' on the grounds that he has been speaking of game birds and has now changed to another kind of game, one with scales instead of feathers. This theory he bases on William Derham's *Physico-Theology* (1713), which devoted a chapter to the wonder of creation in bestowing on each animal a type of clothing exactly suited to its need. Thus *scaly breed* and the *feathered race* are to be distinguished by their garb.[1] But whatever truth there may be in this theory, it could in any case only explain periphrases relating to animals, and what are we to do with *watery plains* and *Phoebus' fiery car*? Any reader who has in his youth struggled with Latin verse composition knows only too well the relief offered by the *Gradus* in solving awkward lines, and almost every periphrasis used by Pope can be traced to the *Gradus* itself. Whilst this does not explain *why* the neo-classicist resorted to periphrasis rather than vivid directness, it does explain fully the means whereby he achieved his circumlocutory effects. And it was a means which came most naturally to a generation of poets nurtured on a diet of Latin verse composition.

Indeed, with his training in Latin versification, the eighteenth-century poet would have needed to make a conscious effort in order to avoid introducing such circumlocutions into his English verse. And in an age which modelled itself on the classical era, the transfer of this device for quantitative verse to the English accentual metre was greatly admired. Lord Kames urged poets to use *the blue vault of heaven* in preference to sky, explaining that '. . . it prevents the object from being brought down by the familiarity of its

[1] G. Tillotson, *On the Poetry of Pope* (Oxford, 1938), p. 77, and his 'Eighteenth Century Poetic Diction', *ES*, xxv (1939). On the use of personification see G. Wilson Knight, *Laureate of Peace* (London, 1954), p. 10. John Arthos in *The Language of Natural Description in Eighteenth Century Poetry* (Ann Arbor, 1949), p. 15, suggests in a footnote that an examination of the *Gradus* might prove valuable in analysing neo-classical verse.

proper name', and James Beattie felt that the substitution of *liquid plain* for *ocean* contributed to poetical harmony.[1]

This periphrastic device, more perhaps than any other single factor, helped to create the distance between the poet and his subject-matter—the generalized abstraction and objectivity which forms the greatest contrast between biblical and neo-classical writing. The *waters* which go up by the mountains and down by the valleys form an infinitely more vivid picture than *the rising Surges* which *spread their op'ning Ranks*, and the device served admirably the neo-classicist's desire to blunt this vividness.

The periphrases in the *Gradus* were followed by a lengthy list of appropriate adjectives, which as a contemporary critic rightly complained, confronted the young versifier with a heap of undistinguished epithets and synonyms before he was mature enough to choose between them.[2] This list did, indeed, lead to their almost random and frequently superfluous use in the English verse of the period. In the best Roman poets, the balance of adjective and noun (a balance emphasized by the inflected endings) could be achieved without unnceessary amplification, and there are no superfluous adjectives in Vergil's haunting description of Charon:

> portitor has *horrendus* aquas et flumina servat
> *terribili* squalore Charon, cui *plurima* mento
> canities *inculta* jacet.

But for a poetaster this technique could be treacherous. In Ambrose Philip's translation of Sappho, the epithets could all be omitted with distinct advantage:

> My Bosom glow'd; the *subtle* Flame
> Ran quick thro' all my *vital* Frame.
> O'er my *dim* Eyes a Darkness hung;
> My Ears with *hollow* Murmurs rung;
> In *dewy* Damps my Limbs were chilled;
> My Blood with *gentle* Horrours thrill'd.[3]

[1] Henry Home (Lord Kames), *Elements of Criticism* (Edinburgh, 1762), xx, vii, 380; and James Beattie, *Essay on Poetry and Musick* (Edinburgh, 1776), p. 533.

[2] Joseph Trapp, *Lectures on Poetry* (London, 1742), p. 73.

[3] Published in *Spectator*, No. 229. The Vergil passage is *Aeneid*, vi, 298; the italics are mine.

The reader might have been allowed to assume that the poet's eyes were dim when darkness hung over them, and there is not even the excuse here of cumulative effect. It is merely that, with his training in Latin versification, he felt that a profusion of epithets lent tone and balance to his poetry.

However, to condemn the Augustan for artificiality and repetition—particularly when we compare him with the vivid and dedicated poet of the Bible—is to misunderstand his purpose, which was not to present a distinctly focused picture nor to share with his reader a powerful emotion, but to start in him a state of mind. All personal experience was to be transmuted into general principles, and in place of Lucy we find 'lovely woman' stooping to folly. The eighteenth-century faith in the uniformity of mankind demanded such generalization, and both personification and a pretended belief in ancient mythology could be exploited for the same ends. The individual submerged himself in abstractions or donned the guise of a mythological figure.

The reason for this dislike of emotional display and its translation into mythological terms lies partially in the cult of wit, one characteristic of which is a fear of ridicule, of making a fool of oneself. The critical tribunal for all Augustan poetry from love-song to satire was something approaching the smoking-room of a modern West End club—scarcely a congenial audience for passionate, self-revelatory verse. In order to forestall potential ridicule, the poet either leapt to the offensive in satire or, if he chose to indulge his softer emotions, he smuggled them in unobtrusively, blunting them by periphrases and mythology.

This restraint and decorum had found its kindred spirit in Horace, in whom there was the same urbanity, wit, and love of what was fit for a gentleman. Many ages have described the glory of dying for one's country, but the highest tribute which Horace could pay was that it was *dulce et decorum*—fitting for a gentleman and therefore desirable. This detached, stoical view of life had its counterpart in the controlled elegies of the eighteenth century, and the contrast with the heartfelt cry of Job illustrates the gulf which lay between the classical and the biblical world. The choice of Horace as the neo-classical model was based, as Miss Goad has explained, on his desire for perfection of form, his commonplaceness, and his lack of romance or ideal above the ordinary, everyday rules of living.[1] For the neo-classical writer, poetry was a social activity which rarely rose above what Dodsley called the merit of '. . . having furnished to the public an elegant and polite Amusement'. Poetry was not equated with amusement, but some didactic quality was required to raise it above that level and it was, in part at least, by a display of erudition—predominantly of classical erudition—that the poet felt he maintained his position as a man of culture.

In recent scholarship there has been a growing tendency to argue for a more truly poetic power in Pope's verse than the mere technical skill and wit traditionally acknowledged. Geoffrey Tillotson, Cleanth Brooks, Maynard Mack and others have enriched our understanding of Pope by revealing the daring and compressed imagery which frequently lies almost concealed beneath the apparently commonplace exterior. Yet their very defence of Pope contains an admission that the calm exterior and reasoned balance which he cultivated in his verse blinds many readers to the more subtle qualities, and in a study of this kind our primary concern must be with the dominant traits despite our readiness to acknowledge the brilliance with which Pope may exploit and counterbalance those more prosaic techniques. Tillotson, for example, reminds us with considerable justice, that in the post-romantic tradition we instinctively compare the eighteenth-century pastoral with romantic nature-poems to the detriment of the former without bothering to acknowledge that the Augustan poet excelled the romantic in poems discussing the relationship between educated man and his fellow-members of society. We unfairly compare the less successful genre of neo-classical

[1] See Caroline M. Goad, *Horace in English Literature of the Eighteenth Century* (New Haven, 1918), and J. W. Johnson, 'The Meaning of *Augustan*', *JHI*, xix (1958).

verse with the best of romantic.[1] The same charge might be levelled against much of the present work, and the *Gradus* technique is certainly more visible in the pastoral than in satire. My intention here, however, is not to establish any final comparative evaluation, but to examine those very aspects of neo-classical writing which were distasteful to the romantic poet, and to watch what steps he took and what models he used to replace, improve, or transform them. In this, the stylized pastoral is clearly of prime significance.

On the other hand, it would be fallacious to imagine that the neo-classical techniques discussed here apply only to the pastoral. A danger inherent in the modern attempt to revalidate neo-classical poetry is that of going too far in the opposite direction. Through a laudable desire to overcome the general reader's prejudices against the 'decorum' and 'intellectualism' of Augustan verse, the critic frequently points out (and rightly so) that such labels obscure the wide variety of style existing between the different genres and even within them. The heroic play, we are reminded, took the Passions as their central theme, satire was exempt from the rules of poetic diction and hence permitted colloquialisms, while the imitations of Ovid's love poetry gave scope for tender searchings of the heart. Now while it is true that a reader immersed in neo-classical poetry becomes aware of subtle variations as he moves from Dryden's heroic plays to Pope's *Windsor Forest*, and from there to *Eloisa* and the satires, the moment he steps back to see them contrasted with the poetry of other ages, their conscious cultivation of rhetorical effect, of calculated artistry, and of sophisticated restraint is at once seen to unite them more effectively than their inner differences divide.

If the neo-classical rules permitted passion in heroic drama, is it passion in the sense of powerful emotion surging from the heart, or is it rather the intellect playing, as it were, with a

---

[1] See Tillotson's article referred to above and Cleanth Brooks, 'The Case of Miss Arabella Fermor' in his *Well Wrought Urn* (New York, 1947), pp. 80 f. Also Maynard Mack, 'Wit and Poetry in Pope' in *Pope and his Contemporaries: Essays Presented to George Sherburn* (Oxford, 1949), pp. 20 f.

hypothetically conceived emotion? The climactic speech of Dryden's *Conquest of Granada* has all the delicate balance, surface paradox, and almost scientific search for definition which we would expect of a philosophical treatise in verse:

> *Abdelmelech (stabbing himself):*
> I do myself that justice I did her.
> That blood I to thy ruined country give,
> But love too well thy murder to outlive.
> Forgive a love excused by its excess,
> Which, had it not been cruel, had been less.
> Condemn my passion, then, but pardon me,
> And think I murdered him who murdered thee. (*Dies.*)

Pope's *Eloisa to Abelard* takes as its theme one of the most moving love stories of history and, within the framework of his own social milieu, he makes of it a gentle Ovidian epistle.

> When from the censer clouds of fragrance roll,
> And swelling organs lift the rising soul,
> One thought of thee puts all the pomp to flight,
> Priests, tapers, temples, swim before my sight:
> In seas of flame, my plunging soul is drown'd,
> While altars blaze, and angels tremble round. . . .

There is brilliant *rhetoric* of passion here, but not passion itself. At no time are we allowed to forget that Pope is speaking on Eloisa's behalf; and this is precisely the effect he wants to achieve. We are meant to admire the general truth that 'swelling organs lift the rising soul' and when Eloisa is made to describe her supposed frenzy, it is not she but her 'plunging soul' which drowns. Not least, as in all heroic couplets of this period, the regular end-stopped lines convey the impression that ultimately all is under control.

Similarly Ian Jack, in his excellent study of Augustan satire, dismisses as absurd the 'threadbare' notion that all Augustan poetry employs poetic diction, insisting that satire does not. He quotes with full approval W. P. Ker's view that Pope's maturer satire, the *Imitations of Horace*, is 'perfectly free' from it.[1] Yet in the very chapter which he himself devotes to the *Imitations* he admits the frequent use in them of an

---

[1] Ian Jack, *Augustan Satire* (Oxford, 1957), pp. 148 and 113.

elevated diction for the purpose of achieving a mock-heroic effect, illustrating with:

> While You, great Patron of Mankind, sustain
> The balanc'd World, and open all the Main.

This substantial exception already accounts for a considerable proportion of the satires. But without entering into quibbles over what is essentially true—that satire permits and encourages colloquialisms—we should not be misled into thinking that those poetic techniques defined above as neo-classical are absent from the satires. In the *Imitations* themselves we open the page at a typical passage, this time without a trace of mock-heroism:

> Whether old age, with faint but cheerful ray,
> Attends to gild the evening of my day,
> Or death's black wing already be display'd
> To wrap me in the universal shade. . . .

The second and last lines might have come straight out of the *Gradus* and the reader needs no assistance in identifying the other obvious neo-classicisms. And lastly let us recall that the example singled out by Wordsworth for attack in his Preface to the *Lyrical Ballads* was not a pastoral by Pope, but an elegiac sonnet by Gray which employs the same *Gradus* forms.

> In vain to me the smiling mornings shine
> And reddening Phoebus lifts his golden fire:
> The birds in vain their amorous descant join,
> Or cheerful fields resume their green attire. . . .

For all the differences, therefore, which exist between and within the neo-classical genres, there are certain common aspects of mood, tone, and, not least, of mechanical techniques which unify them despite their diversity. And it was to those very techniques that the poets of the following generation objected. Since it was largely in the realm of nature poetry that the romantic felt the difference most keenly, I have tended to lay more stress upon pastoral. However, any impression that such comments apply exclusively to the pastoral should be more than offset by the large number of illustrations drawn from contemporary paraphrases of the Bible. For the latter ought, by their subject-matter, to have evoked as passionate a form of writing as the neo-classicist was capable of. That it resulted almost invariably in circumlocution, detachment, and diffusion is sufficient indication that these stylistic devices had permeated almost the entire body of Augustan verse.

We began by comparing passages typical of biblical and neo-classical verse, and it may be useful to conclude in the same way in order to check the validity of the contrasts suggested. But this time we may go even further by comparing a biblical passage with an eighteenth-century versification of it to show how the neo-classicist felt impelled to clothe the Bible in the garb of Augustan diction in order to make poetry of it.

In answer to Job's passionate pleas for justice, God's voice from the whirlwind drives home question after question to impress Job with the petty insignificance of man.

Canst thou draw out leviathan with an hook? Or his tongue with a cord which thou lettest down? Canst thou put a hook into his nose? Or bore his jaw through with a thorn? Will he make supplications unto thee? Will he speak soft words unto thee? Will he make a covenant with thee? Wilt thou take him for a servant for ever? Wilt thou play with him as with a bird? Or wilt thou bind him for thy maidens?

For this, Edward Young has

Go to the Nile, and, from its fruitful side,
Cast forth thy line into the swelling tide:
With slender hair leviathan command,
And stretch his vastness on the loaded strand.
Will he become thy servant? Will he own
Thy lordly nod and tremble at thy frown?
Or with his sport amuse thy leisure day,
And, bound in silk, with thy soft maidens play?[1]

Again the contrast is between vivid, fervent identification on the one hand, and detached, controlled rhetoric on the other. The effect is produced by precisely the same technique as in the earlier comparison. The 'unpoetic' words *hook*, *jaw* and *thorn* are replaced by delicate periphrases such as *com-*

[1] Job xli, 1, and Edward Young, *Poetical Works* (London, 1834), ii, 185.

manding the leviathan *with slender hair* from the *swelling tide*;
the participial epithet of the *loaded* strand contains a mildly
witty compression of meaning; and the concrete biblical image
play with him as with a bird is replaced by the more generalized
with his sport amuse thy leisure day. The total effect is that the
sharp picture of man's puny efforts to subdue the monster is
blurred to become the conventional eighteenth-century landscape painting of the angler calmly fishing by the stream,
acknowledging that the leviathan is a trifle too heavy for his
fishing-rod, and somewhat too cumbersome for a pet. The
irony, the scorn and the urgency of the biblical questions has
evaporated completely.

The relegation of poetry to the status of an amusement for
the leisured classes lies at the opposite pole to its function in
the Bible. The biblical world-picture, which integrated all
aspects of human life and oriented them towards their ultimate
purpose—the service of God, made each of those aspects
potentially holy. Literature itself had a sacred function to
perform, and one which raised it to the level of a priestly task.
The songs and lyrics of the Bible were sung as the Levites
ascended the steps of the Temple, its laments were for the fall
of the holy city, its heroes were the patriarchs and the kings
anointed with holy oil, and its didactic poems were to teach
men the paths of righteousness. Throughout its literature is
felt the purposefulness of existence, moving from creation
towards the messianic fulfilment of prophecy; and the function of the prophets themselves was to keep that messianic
hope before the eyes of the people and to foster the righteousness which would hasten its fulfilment.

This is a far cry from neo-classical verse, and it is, perhaps,
scarcely fair even to make comparisons. Within its narrower
field, Augustan poetry fulfilled its purpose admirably. What
does concern us, however, is that romantic poetry stood closer
to the prophetic tradition, catching fire from its sparks. To
give but one example, the high seriousness of poetry is never
felt so strongly in English literature as it is in Milton, whose
biblical theme sanctified what might have been no more than
an Arthurian epic. But the next in rank to Milton among those

who felt the lofty solemnity of their poetic duties was Wordsworth, who had no religious theme (at least in the conventional sense) to justify his feeling of dedication. In relating his own poetic beginnings—a tradition borrowed from the biblical call to service of Moses, Samuel and Isaiah—Wordsworth relates how

> . . . poetic numbers came
> Spontaneously, and cloth'd in priestly robe
> My spirit, thus singled out, as it might seem,
> For holy services.[1]

Poetry had now become a holy service, however secular its theme. And one of those 'holy services' for which Wordsworth felt he had been singled out was his account in the *Prelude* of the growth of poetic genius.

But how had this change in the status of poetry been effected, a change from its being a polite amusement to being a holy duty? We have said that next to Milton Wordsworth ranked highest in his sense of lofty purpose; but between the two stood Blake, a poet so profoundly identified with the biblical prophetic tradition that he scarcely seems conscious that poetry could have any function other than that of conveying a divine message. And it is through the pre-romantics that this rise in the status of poetry may be traced.

Between neo-classicism and romanticism a change had occurred which was closely in line with the biblical tradition. For in place of the wit, the stylization, the balance and the restraint of early eighteenth-century verse, the romantic poet, spurning the poetic diction of the preceding generation, was turning from the form to the spirit, from classicism to Hebraism. The struggle involved was recorded by Wordsworth himself. He strove to free himself from all those traditions established by the *Gradus* technique and the other concomitants of the worship of form.

---

[1] Wordsworth, *Prelude* (1805), i, 60, ed. E. de Selincourt (Oxford, 1926), p. 4. It is worth noting that when Wordsworth did find a conventionally religious theme after 1807 his poetry deteriorated. Grierson touches upon the prophetic aspects of Wordsworth in his *Milton and Wordsworth* (London, 1956).

In general terms
I was a better judge of thoughts than words,
Misled as to these latter not alone
By common inexperience of youth
But by the trade in classic niceties,
Delusion to young scholars incident
And old ones also, by that overpriz'd
And dangerous craft of picking phrases out
From languages that want the living voice.[1]

His training in the craft of 'picking phrases' out of Latin handbooks as a young scholar had so deeply impressed him, as it had his immediate predecessors and contemporaries, that it was difficult to break through the heavy curtain of poetic diction and periphrasis to convey vividly and effectively the impulses of the heart rather than of the mind.

Poetry itself stood at the parting of the ways. The road it had been travelling was the road of Reason. Here the classics had been the guide, offering a model both chaste and elegant. Verse appeared for the most part in the balanced, regular form of the heroic couplet, achieving its effect by the wit of circumlocution, of bathos, and of delicate allusion. Poetry was the gentleman's pastime, aiming at expressing general truths with charm and taste, often in the garb of classical mythology. The new road branching off from this was the road of passionate individualism, which scorned stylistic embellishments and demanded the language of the heart. It was a road in which nature was to become glorious and yet awesome, in which the broad daylight and the company of human society was often to be exchanged for mysterious darkness and romantic solitude. And it is the purpose of this study to examine the way in which the Old Testament, itself an ancient, oriental work, fostered the movements of primitivism and orientalism; and how, with the magic of its poetry, its knowledge of the human heart, its newly discovered freedom from metrical forms, and the reverence in which it was held, it helped to protect the poetic innovator from abuse as he left Reason behind him and turned towards romanticism.

[1] Ibid., vi, 123, in ed. cit., p. 176.

2

The Laminated Bible

The rising interest in Old Testament poetry during the eighteenth century suggests that its literary merits had not been fully appreciated before then. The Authorized Version had, indeed, been acclaimed as a masterpiece, but people came very slowly to think of the Bible as a literary work. It was a divinely inspired guide for moral conduct, and a holy source-book for Christianity. To view it as literature seemed almost profane.

However, this unwillingness to apply literary criteria to the Bible had deeper roots. For in the Middle Ages, the Old Testament had been regarded not as the chronicles of the ancient Hebrews, the literary record of their aspirations, backslidings, and moral vision, but as a prelude to the New Testament, holy only insofar as it foretold the coming of the Christian Messiah. Commentary on it became restricted almost exclusively to a search beneath the literal text for those prefigurative allusions to the Gospels which it was thought to conceal. The story of Abraham's sacrifice became a foreshadowing of the Father allowing the blood of his only begotten Son to be shed, the faggots which Isaac bears on his shoulder symbolizing the wooden Cross.

In fact, the entire Bible was viewed as a series of cyclical repetitions both of the Crucifixion and of broader Christian themes. A twelfth-century playlet, the *Ordo de Ysaac et Rebecca et Filiis Eorum*, for example, inserts after every scene from the story of Isaac a chorus explaining the true meaning to the audience. Esau, we are told, represents the Jews who followed the letter instead of the spirit of the Law, while

Jacob symbolizes the Christian community, younger in years but greater in faith. The Christians earn by this faith the blessing of the firstborn and hence inherit from the Jews the right to be God's chosen people. As Esau won his father's love by supplying him with tasty venison, so the Hebrews had won divine favour by their animal sacrifices; and the clothes left behind by Esau are the Decalogue neglected by the Jews and adopted by their successors. The questionable theology involved in allowing God to be 'deceived' by animal sacrifices and the very identification of Christianity with Jacob in an action of doubtful morality appear not to have troubled the allegorists unduly; for the entire system of prefigurative interpretation had become so central a part of medieval Christian thought that it seemed sacrilegious even to question it.[1] Typology offered the Christian preacher a host of colourful stories beloved by the people and used by him to impart the teachings of the Christian faith. Jonah and the whale, Adam and Eve, Samson and Delilah, gazed down from the frescoes and stained-glass windows in the Church side by side with scenes from the Nativity and Crucifixion, and, so far from distracting from the latter scenes, they now served to confirm that the events recorded in the Gospels had been ordained from the beginnings of Creation.

This cyclical interpretation was, moreover, no chance mannerism; it reflected the basic philosophy of the age. In the vision of the world *sub specie aeternitatis*, reality was only to be found after death, and the events of this world became telescoped as one gazed steadfastly towards the world to come. On a thirteenth-century marble pulpit in Pisa, Nicholas Pisano portrayed the Annunciation and the Nativity as though they had occurred simultaneously, and in the liturgical drama Joseph in Egypt stood three paces away from his

[1] In Karl Young, *The Drama of the Medieval Church* (Oxford, 1933), ii, 260. The Bible itself recognized the immorality of Jacob's act by punning on his name, 'he has *deceived* me these two times', in an age when names reflected character. The pun is, of course, lost in the English translation. On typology in general, see Basil Smalley, *The Study of the Bible in the Middle Ages* (Oxford, 1952) and Helen Gardner, *The Limits of Literary Criticism* (Oxford, 1956).

brethren in Palestine with no attempt on the part of actor or producer to suggest the distance which separated them. If God rode on the wings of the wind and a thousand years in His sight were but as yesterday, what need was there to be concerned with a few hundred miles or the passing of ten generations! The objections of a modern reader to the anachronism of finding Christ in Samson would have sounded hollow in the ears of a medieval scholar, concerned with the spiritual world which lay beyond reality.

Officially, the text of the Old Testament contained for the scholiast a laminated pattern of four equally valid meanings.

> Littera gesta docet,
> Quid credas allegoria,
> Moralis quid agas,
> Quo tendas anagogia.[1]

In practice, however, three of these four meanings were generally ignored. The literal story was regarded as an almost valueless husk, homily was reserved largely for New Testament exegesis, while the anagogical method deteriorated into the mystic interpretation of numbers, far removed from the narrative itself. The commentator was left with the task of uncovering the allegorical sense—the kernel within the husk. Nor was this allegorical principle restricted to such thematic parallels as the betrayals of Samson and Christ, but was pursued with extraordinary rigour even into the minutiae of the text. Augustine set the tone by the ingenuity with which he milked dry the symbolic possibilities of the biblical narrative. In his *City of God* he interpreted Noah's Ark itself as a symbol of Christ on the grounds that the length of the human body, like the dimensions of the Ark, is six times its breadth, and with this proved he could draw parallels between these two Redeemers of mankind. Typological interpretation became a central part of medieval theology with the assistance of such reference works as Strabo's *Glossa Ordinaria* and the

---

[1] A much older jingle quoted in the preface to the polyglot Complutensian Bible (Alcala, 1520). See also H. Flanders Dunbar, *Symbolism in Medieval Thought* (New Haven, 1929), p. 31.

Allegoria in Vetus Testamentum attributed to Hugo of St. Victor. There any reader or preacher could look up a biblical story to find the deeper, symbolic meanings which it contained. The literal narrative was almost ignored.

The persistence of this prefigurative method can be gauged from its prominence in the Geneva Version of the Bible, published in 1560, in which the chapter headings appear to those unacquainted with this method totally unrelated to the contents of the chapter they head. To take an example at random, Psalm lxix, a plea by King David for divine assistance in time of personal trouble and to the modern reader apparently devoid of any Christological allusions, is introduced:

1. The complaints, prayers, fervent zeale & great anguish of David is set forth as a figure of Christ & all his members. 21. The malicious crueltie of the enemies, 22. and their punishement also. 26. Where Judas and suche traitors are accursed. . . . 35. Finally he doeth prouoke all creatures to praises, prophecying of the Church, where all the faithful 37 and their sede shall dwell for euer.

So long as the Old Testament was regarded merely as the harbinger of the New, as a dark prophecy pointing forward to the Christian Messiah, it could not be judged as the divinely inspired literature of the primitive Hebrews, wrought out of the vivid experiences of a nation almost obsessed by its consciousness of right and wrong. And until it was so regarded, it could not serve as a literary model for later poets seeking the more exotic writings of 'oriental climes'.

Huizinga has remarked that the battle-cry of sixteenth-century humanism was *Ad fontes!* and in the realm of biblical exegesis it was this insistence on a return to sources which distinguished the early Reformers even when they remained loyal members of the Catholic Church. Reuchlin had no intention of undermining the authority of Rome when he claimed that the Hebrew original of the Old Testament was more reliable than the Vulgate, but his philological researches proved to be a major step towards the Protestant Reformation. For it was not mere linguistic ignorance which had caused the Hebrew Bible to be neglected during the Middle Ages. It was also the conviction expressed, among others by

Nicolaus of Lyra, that the Jews had deliberately falsified their texts in order to confuse and confute the Christian. It took longer than Reuchlin's lifetime to overcome this suspicion of Jewish sources, and he complained bitterly towards the end of his days that he had become 'as it were the protomartyr of Hebrew letters, sacrificed, tortured, burned, torn to pieces, and lacerated'.[1] Behind the theological elements in the translation dispute, therefore, can be perceived, perhaps as a concomitant rather than a cause, a tendency to exchange the conventional medieval picture of Jews as corruptors and deniers for a more sympathetic recognition that they were, after all, the direct descendants of the Old Testament figures, and thus in a sense closer to the original sources.

Nevertheless, the new interest in Hebrew might have remained purely academic were it not for that growing sense of identification with the Hebrew patriarchs, prophets, and poets discernible in the Protestant Reformation. The Reformers' demand for an open Bible and for its translation into the vernacular led inevitably to a fresh appraisal of Old Testament narrative. Instead of confession and absolution at the hands of a priest, they sought direct communion with God, and in place of a Latin Bible interpreted by the Church, they demanded a translation which they could read and interpret for themselves.

The free access to the Bible which such translation provided brought with it a renewed interest in the stories of the Old Testament. They could now be read in their original form and not merely be heard of in the allegorical interpretations of the preachers. We sometimes forget that the vast majority of people in the Middle Ages only knew their Bible at second hand. A nobleman, trying to argue with a cleric in 1143, can only rely upon hearsay even when discussing the simplest biblical story:

[1] J. Huizinga, *Erasmus of Rotterdam*, tr. F. Hopman (London, 1952) p. 109. For a general account of the sixteenth-century debate, see W. Schwarz, *Principles and Problems of Biblical Translation* (Cambridge, 1955), and for a brief summary of the following century's interpretation of the Scriptures, Basil Willey's *Seventeenth Century Background* (New York, 1955), chapter iv.

Now you talk to me again of Lot and his wife, whom I have never seen or known. . . . But I have heard say that an angel commanded them to leave the city where they had dwelt and not to look back, and because the woman looked back, she was changed into a statue of salt.[1]

By the end of the sixteenth century there were several English translations to choose from, and there was no excuse for not knowing one's Bible in a literal translation of the original text.

However, there was a further reason for the Protestant's interest in the Old Testament. As we have seen, the Catholic Church had always maintained that the Christians were the newly chosen people of God, inheriting that right from the Jews at the moment when they denied Christ. Indeed the Gospels themselves had made the point:

Come ye blessed of my father, inherit the kingdom prepared for you from the foundation of the earth (Matthew xxv, 34).

Nevertheless, the Catholics had always assumed that the covenant had been passed on to the body of the Church, represented by its Pope. The Protestant, and particularly the Calvinist, in order to circumvent the medieval authority of Rome, insisted that the covenant had been made initially with one individual—Abraham—and had been renewed with Isaac and Jacob in order to show that for all its communal features, ultimately the divine covenant was established with each individual Christian. The grace of God had been bestowed upon his elect, the new 'seed of Abraham', and the sinner was to plead for forgiveness not through the Church by means of indulgences and pardons, but directly to his God on the basis of his covenant. To confirm his trust in ultimate salvation, the Protestant read eagerly of God's promises to the Hebrew patriarchs, of the reaffirmation of the covenant from generation to generation, and he felt himself to be part of that spiritual family of which the patriarchs were the founders. No longer was the Old Testament merely a series of Christological prefigurations. It had become in addition the exciting history of the progressive revelation of the covenant, a covenant

[1] H. W. C. Davies, 'Henry of Blois and Brian Fitz-Count', *EHR*, xxv (1910), quoted in Smalley, op. cit., p. xiv.

which possessed a peculiarly personal significance for the Protestant.

Typology continued, if in a weakened form, but parallel with it was a renewed interest in the literal stories themselves, and especially in such stories as that of Joseph, unjustly condemned to imprisonment but eventually redeemed by the grace of God because he was of the Chosen Seed.[1] The sixteenth-century Protestant, hunted and reviled by the established Church, found comfort and faith in such tales, frequently translating the contemporary scene into a biblical setting in which he was identified with the biblical hero, and his enemies with the unrighteous whom God would overthrow. Later, in the same tradition, Cromwell's troops sang the Psalms of David as they marched into battle against the 'Philistines', and Milton saw himself as Samson, eyeless in Gaza.

In the realm of biblical criticism, the revival of interest in the biblical narrative, in the simple stories themselves rather than their allegorical meaning, did not usurp the place of traditional exegesis at once, and the medieval insistence on the prefigurative sense continued to predominate. In 1619, George Wither still asserted dogmatically that there was nothing in the Old Testament written for its own sake, but that all narrative, commandments, and histories were parables to figure out what should be fulfilled in the coming of the Messiah; and he attacks the ordinary reader because

. . . when any of the learned *Poets* have the ill fortune to fall into their hands, they look onely into the Historicall part of the Worke; and being unable to crack the shell that couers the sweet kernell, like Swine they feed on huskes . . ., they . . . are ignorant of the *Allegoricall* sense of the Psalmes and other Bookes of holy Scriptures.

The fact that he castigates some readers for enjoying the husk instead of the kernel indicates that a change was already occurring, and a few years later John Selden championed the literalist view by vigorously condemning the Church Fathers

[1] Cf. Leicester Bradner, 'The Latin Drama of the Renaissance', *Studies in the Renaissance*, iv (1957).

for pursuing allegories before they had understood the literal text. The vivid metaphor he employs contains the germs of the new empirical method.

Here at ye first sight appears to me in my window a glasse and a booke; thereupon I goe about to tell you what they Signifie; Afterwards upon nearer view they prove noe Such things; one is a Box made like a booke the other is a picture made like a Glasse; where's now my Allegory.[1]

Perhaps the best illustration of the shift in viewpoint is the changing attitude to the *Song of Songs*. For the seventeenth-century scholar, John Collinges, it was no less than 'the intercourse of divine love betwixt Christ and the Church' with the Shulamite maiden serving as no more than a symbol. Collinges would no doubt have been scandalized to know that a century later the same work would be described as 'one of the most beautiful pastorals in the world' which had been unnecessarily obscured by those '. . . busily employed in opening and unfolding its allegorical meaning'.[2]

Selden's rejection of the old view, Robert Boyle's concern with what the ancient Hebrews had made of the supposed Christological references,[3] and indeed the general awakening of interest in what the Old Testament actually said rather than what it was supposed to mean, form part of that move away from belief in ghosts and witches towards rational enquiry. These dark prefigurements smacked of mystery and medieval shibboleth distasteful to the empiricists of the new scientific age. Selden's example of the optical illusion, which could have been rectified by the simple expedient of taking a closer look, revealed a tendency to apply scientific criteria to medieval dogma. It was a sign that Bacon's dichotomy of scientific and religious truth would no longer hold good.

[1] George Wither, *A Preparation to the Psalter* (*1619*) (London, 1884), p. 104, and John Selden, *Table Talk*, ed. F. Pollock (London, 1927), p. 12. Although the latter work was originally published in 1689, it records conversations of an earlier period.

[2] From the title of John Collinges' translation of *Canticles*, ii (London, 1676), and the preface to Thomas Percy's version of the whole *Song* published in London in 1764.

[3] R. Boyle, *Some Considerations Touching the Style of the Holy Scriptures* (London, 1661), p. 37.

The consequent turning towards the literal meaning of the text was intensified, to some extent fortuitously, by the publication of the Authorized Version itself. When, at the Hampton Court conference of 1604, John Rainolds first suggested the project to King James, the latter insisted that no marginal notes should be added to the text. He had seen in the Geneva Version how such marginal notes could be exploited for purely sectarian purposes; in consequence the Authorized Version restricted its notes almost entirely to linguistic explanations and its page headings to brief summaries of the literal meaning of the text. However, while the purpose of this caveat had been to avoid denominational propagandizing, the net result was an invitation to the reader to see what the text itself had to say. The Bible was presented stripped of its allegorical encrustations and bare of medieval commentary, so that the Old Testament itself appeared not as a prefigurative foreshadowing of the New but as the earlier history of the covenant, as the history of the Hebrews recorded by themselves and hence as the literature of an ancient civilization. As such, the poet could consider it stylistically and begin to model his own verse upon its literary techniques.

This concern with the literal meaning of the Bible and the distaste for the mysteries of typology was a change in sensibility closely connected with that desire for 'perspicuity' which became a hallmark of the new critical school. Johnson's attack upon the metaphysical poets for the abstruseness of their metaphors marked the culmination of a growing desire to come to grips with the simple meaning of a text or an idea without having to unravel metaphorical obscurities, and the new ideal for poetry was, as Dryden put it, 'to mould thoughts into easy, significant words, in which the rhyme should never mislead the sense but itself be led and governed by it'.[1] The simple sense, as opposed to any deeper allegorical meaning had now become a primary ingredient of good verse.

Indeed, this change in biblical criticism was summarized in the new epithet, applied to the Bible so frequently during this

---

[1] *Of Dramatic Poesy* in *Essays of John Dryden*, ed. W. P. Ker (Oxford, 1926), i, 35.

period that it was to become a mere cliché. Scarcely a comment was made on the literary merit of the Bible at the turn of the century which did not contain some reference to its noble *simplicity*, and it was a term which could not have been used meaningfully before the seventeenth century. For it suggested a deliberate ignoring of the allegorical tradition, and an assessment based entirely upon the literal meaning and expression of the text. Moreover, it was a term ideally suited to the interests of the primitivist, and one which allowed him to establish parallels with the ancient simplicity of Homer so that on the authority of these two revered works he could begin to break away from the more stylized forms of neo-classical literature.

At this stage, a fundamental problem arose for the biblical critic, but one of which he appears to have been only subconsciously aware. The mass of critical writing in the seventeenth and eighteenth centuries abounds, as every student of the period knows, with bold assertions of the superiority of the Scriptures over the classics of Greece and Rome, and, what is more remarkable, these statements are made dogmatically— one might almost say belligerently—as though in the teeth of powerful opposition. To give but one example, Robert Boyle's *Some Considerations Touching the Style of the Holy Scriptures* (1661) is devoted almost in its entirety to answering the various attacks which might be made upon the literary merit of the Bible. Yet when we look for these attacks or indeed for any kind of opposition to the literary claims made for the Bible, they are almost non-existent. Boyle, it is true, quotes with ridicule the story of an Englishman who '. . . solemnly preferred one of the Odes of Pindarus before all the Psalms of David' but even this in its context reads like a fabrication invented in order to be knocked down. Why, then, are the advocates of Hebrew literature so keen to answer an apparently non-existent attack?

The opposition they were attempting to stifle was, I would suggest, the still, small voice of their own conscience, and the key to much of the biblical criticism of this period lies in the sense of 'guilt' which the critics felt. They knew instinctively that the divine writings ought, by their very nature, to excel human compositions. But since they did not yet understand the character of Hebrew poetry, that it depended upon parallelism and not upon an accentual or quantitative metre, they found themselves trying to assess its literary merit by the yardstick of classical literature; and the results proved disappointing. If Shakespeare offended against the neo-classical rules, readers were requested to make some allowance for his ignorance since in Shakespeare's day the English nation was still struggling to emerge from barbarity.[1] But the sanctity of the Holy Scriptures precluded such extenuations. Their excellence over all other compositions was assumed as an unquestionable fact, but how to prove it by neo-classical rules was a very different problem. The critic (if only rarely) had to admit '. . . 'tis more modest and becoming to lay the fault on our own ignorance, if we don't see that Beauty and Elegance which the antient Hebrews did'.[2] Until the different principles of Hebrew poetry had been explained, and until the new view had arisen that the Bible was the literature of a primitive people, a literature free from the trammels of classical style, and to be judged by different literary standards, the critics could only drown their doubts in repeated assertions of the literary supremacy of the Bible. And like the lady who insisted that she had never borrowed her neighbour's pots and had in any case already returned them, they bolstered their own assertions of biblical supremacy by adding a host of excuses and apologies for the literary inadequacies of the Bible.

One frequent and, to a certain extent, justified 'excuse' for the Bible was that translation had obscured the merit of the original. The Augustan translator was, in general, inclined to pour foreign works into neo-classical moulds and then marvel how far the translation proved the original to have conformed to the 'rules'. But whatever the translator might do, the reader still had by his side (or rather by heart) an officially authorized version of the Bible which gave the literal meaning of the original. For many eighteenth-century readers Homer

[1] Samuel Johnson, *Preface to Shakespeare* (1765).
[2] J. Stennet, *A Version of Solomon's Song* (London, 1709), pp. xii–xiii.

was what Pope had made him, but the English translation of the Bible had forestalled such Procrustean work on the Holy Scriptures. The critic, in order to explain away the Bible's non-conformity to the rules, was left to assume that something had disappeared in the process of translation. Sir William Temple thought it particularly praiseworthy that the Song of Deborah retained much of its nobility despite its translation into 'so common Prose', and even such enthusiastic advocates of biblical literature as Boyle and (later) Husbands felt it necessary to offer the usual apologies for the literary defects of the English Bible.[1]

On this point, Addison with his usual critical acumen, revealed a deeper understanding than his contemporaries. Instead of blaming the translation, he realized that the Bible withstood literal translation far better than the classics. He advised his readers to compare the stylistic absurdity of a literal version of Horace or Pindar with the splendours of the English Psalter and to observe '. . . how kindly the *Hebrew* manners of speech mix and incorporate with the English language'.[2] To offer any explanation of this difference was beyond Addison's powers, for it required a knowledge of parallelism, and the new theory had not yet been expounded. For the classical poet, by depending upon a metrical rhythm, balanced couplets, and most important of all, such verbal juxtaposition as can be permitted only in an inflected language is left with almost nothing in translation. One of Horace's most famous odes literally translated would read:

I abhor the irreverent mob and keep them at a distance. Keep silent! As priest of the Muses, I recite a new ode for girls and boys.

What a difference from the sparkling original!

Odi profanum vulgus et arceo;
favete linguis: carmina non prius
audita Musarum sacerdos
virginibus puerisque canto.[3]

---

[1] Sir William Temple, *Of Poetry* in J. E. Spingarn, *Critical Essays of the Seventeenth Century* (Oxford, 1908–9), iii, 87; Boyle, op. cit., p. 162; and Husbands, *Preface to the Miscellany of Poems* (1731).

[2] *Spectator*, No. 405.   [3] Horace, *Odes*, iii, 1.

But the biblical poet has, as we have seen, only a loose metrical requirement to satisfy, the main rhythm being one of sense, which comes across in translation leaving comparatively little behind. Isaiah is infinitely more effective than Horace in a literal prose version.

And there shall come forth a rod out of the stem of Jesse, and a branch shall grow out of his roots. And the spirit of the Lord shall rest upon him, the spirit of wisdom and understanding, the spirit of counsel and might, the spirit of knowledge and of the fear of the Lord.

However, until parallelism had been explained, the door to a real understanding of Hebrew verse was closed, and one could do little more than peer through the keyhole.

Among other excuses for the Bible, one ingenious method of avoiding the issue was to maintain that the Greeks and Romans had modelled their writings upon the Bible. It was a theory devoid of historical foundation, although it served a useful purpose; for if the classics did appear in any way to excel the Scriptures, the latter still retained the credit. Anthony Blackwall, for example, maintained that the descent of the Homeric gods in human form in order to converse with mortals was copied from God's walking in Paradise and discoursing with Adam and Eve.[1] Apart from the lack of historicity, this theory indicates a lamentable insensitivity to the almost casual mythological interest of the one and the awesome significance of the other.

The seventeenth-century acknowledgement, felt if not expressed, of the inferiority of biblical style to its sublime content was, perhaps, best illustrated in Milton's poetry. For, although he took the subject-matter for much of his poetry, and frequently his imagery, directly from the Bible, he was compelled to turn to classical epic or to Greek drama for the form in which it should be cast. Like Jerome, his admiration for classical poetry was checked by his contempt for the pagan deities to whom it was consecrated, and Milton felt the incongruity of having to turn to the pagans for literary guidance.

[1] A. Blackwall, *An Introduction to the Classics* (London, 1725), p. 82.

Like so many of his contemporaries, he resorts to the hackneyed suggestion that the Greeks must have been indebted to the Bible for their artistry (although he does not explain why he cannot find such literary artistry in the Bible itself).

> Our Hebrew Songs and Harps in *Babylon*
> That pleased so well our Victors ears, declare
> That rather *Greece* from us these arts deriv'd
> Ill imitated, while they loudest sing
> The vices of thir Deities, and thir own
> In Fable, Hymn or Song, so personating
> Thir gods ridiculous and themselves past shame.[1]

On the other hand, his love of scriptural writing lacked an understanding of its metrical form, and in the combination of scriptural subject-matter and classical verse-form lay the cornerstone of his success. In his invocation at the beginning of *Paradise Lost*

> Sing, Heavenly Muse, that on the secret top
> Of Oreb, or of Sinai, didst inspire
> That Shepherd who first taught the Chosen Seed . . .

he instinctively used the classical term *Muse* to address the biblical Spirit of divine inspiration—a paradox inherited from Du Bartas's *La Muse Chrestiene* (1574). Both poets were eager to demonstrate the literary supremacy of the Bible, but found it necessary to resort to classical form in the process.[2]

In this same tradition we find repeated references to the great themes which could be borrowed from the Bible, with only passing hints at the literary form. It was assumed that those biblical themes possessed a transcendent validity which would compensate for any stylistic inferiority and that 'the meanest Christian, however he may fail in diction, is able to surpass the noblest wits of antiquity in the truth and greatness of his sentiments'.[3] Yet the fact that Prior found Proverbs

---

[1] *Paradise Regained*, iv, 336.

[2] See G. C. Taylor, *Milton's Use of Du Bartas* (Cambridge, Mass., 1934), and David Daiches, 'The Opening of *Paradise Lost*' in *The Living Milton*, ed. Frank Kermode (London, 1960), p. 64.

[3] H. Felton, *Dissertation on Reading the Classics* (London, 1713), p. 166.

(which is already in verse) a storehouse of prudential morality for didactic poems, and that Addison thought Psalm xix excellent poetic material when it was already poetry in the Hebrew, shows that critics felt that these passages needed to be refashioned before they could pass the contemporary test of poetry.[1]

That the critics felt uneasy at being unable to perceive the literary merit of the Bible is amply confirmed by a close examination of the eulogies of Scripture which are scattered throughout the critical writings of the age. Milton insists that the Hebrew songs and hymns 'may be easily made appear over all the kinds of Lyric poesy to be incomparable', Blackwell assures us that 'it would be no difficult matter' for a man of taste and learning to prove the superiority of the Bible over classical literature, and Addison feels convinced that such superiority 'might easily be shewn, if there were occasion for it'. But where, among all these commendations, is any serious attempt made to prove the point?

It was certainly easier to assume proof than to attempt the task of probing deeply into the literary character of Holy Writ, particularly when there was no accepted theory to explain the nature of Hebrew verse. The frequent laudations of Scripture in this period give an impression of enlightened appreciation and discriminating criticism, but in fact the overwhelming majority of such criticism was vague, repetitive and devoid of analytical method. Boyle was a comparatively enlightened biblical critic who had demanded a distinction between the plain sense of the text and those metaphysical subtleties which theologians had fathered upon it; yet he had little to say of the Scriptures themselves other than to admire '. . . the Beauty, the Symmetry and the Magnificence of the Structure'; Cowley describes parts of the Bible as '. . . most admirable and exalted pieces of Poesie'; and Pope echoes his predecessors in admiring the 'majestic simplicity'. The terms *grandeur*, *majesty*, *beauty* and *simplicity* occur throughout these criticisms with monotonous reiteration and, by frequently being joined to comments on the divinity of the

[1] Preface to Prior's *Solomon* (1718) and *Spectator*, No. 465.

work, corroborate the view that they were being used to camouflage an ignorance of which the critics were only sub-consciously aware—an ignorance of those basic differences between Hebrew and classical verse outlined above.

Indeed, throughout these passages quoted there is scarcely one illustration of the argument. At a time when the classics were sifted through and through for illustrations of allegory, of rhetorical questions, of turns of phrase, and even for the use of exclamation marks, the disinclination of biblical critics to apply the same diligence to the Scriptures is indicative of their desire to admire merely from the distance. This reluctance to approach too closely arose partly from their ignorance of parallelism and partly from the fear that the suspicion which they were trying to stifle—the suspicion that the Bible was not stylistically comparable to the classics—might be proved true.

The transformation of this hesitancy into an enthusiastic exploration of biblical literature was at first gradual, but gathered momentum so quickly that by the mid-eighteenth century its work was almost complete. In its earlier stages one has the impression that the critic, unused to considering the Bible linguistically, was groping blindly towards some essential distinction between classical and scriptural style; but even that was an improvement on the vague epithets of his predecessors. Addison, discussing the debt of the English language to the Bible, felt the warmth and force infused into English idiom by Hebrew phraseology but made no attempt to analyse the stylistic cause. 'How cold and dead', he exclaims, 'does a Prayer appear, that is composed in the most Elegant and Polite Forms of Speech, which are natural to our Tongue, when it is not heightened by that Solemnity of Phrase which may be drawn from the Sacred Writings.' He does not question whether the elegant and polite forms of speech are suitable as the language of the spirit, nor does he suggest why the phrases borrowed from the sacred writings fire the soul. His colleague Steele, impressed by the magnificent horse image in Job, seemed on the brink of defining a fundamental technique of scriptural imagery. He perceived the difference

57

between what he termed the 'inward principle' of biblical imagery and the purely external depiction of neo-classical verse. He had almost grasped the distinction between the detached observation of the Augustan and the personal involvement of the scriptural poet, but he stopped short and ended his analysis with the usual uncritical panegyric of the 'immortal' authors.[1]

If the critic had not as yet effectively analysed Hebraic literature, he was at least increasingly concerned with its stylistic and poetic qualities. Aaron Hill's famous preface to *Creation* (1720) did more than merely advocate an imitation of the Bible; it selected for especial praise the 'magnificent Plainness' and concrete suggestiveness of its imagery—two qualities which contrasted vividly with the periphrastic 'decency' of contemporary verse. John Husbands' fiery defence of Hebrew poetry was more than a plea for the use of scriptural themes. It insisted that the Bible was divine in its language as well as in its spiritual message and deserved to be selected as a new model for poetry. The climate of opinion had, therefore, already become more congenial to imitation of the Bible when Lowth's lectures provided that concrete analysis towards which the critics had been groping. And perhaps no less important than his parallelist theory was his new technique of illustrating every literary comment with a host of apt illustrations. Where previous critics had unconsciously shied away from illustrative quotation because their own critical theories were as yet too vague to withstand close application, Lowth's insistence on ample illustration displayed the author's conviction that biblical literature would stand up to the closest scrutiny and the most careful comparison with classical writers. Moreover, it directed the reader's attention to the text of the Bible itself and away from those neo-classical verse paraphrases which had commonly been accepted as the most effective proof of the Bible's literary supremacy. And with this bold assertion of the efficacy of the Scriptures as literature, the old allegorical method was left behind, still to be pursued for some years by the theologians but by now

[1] *Spectator*, No. 405, and *Guardian*, No. 86.

practically ignored by the literary world. The way in which this closer examination of the Bible revealed its literary merits and suggested its candidacy as a poetic model forms the subject of the following chapters. At all events, by the end of the eighteenth century the literalist (and hence literary) approach had won the day. J. D. Michaelis, the German orientalist, scoffed at the allegorists for inventing theories utterly foreign to the mind of the biblical poet; Percy's version of the *Song of Songs* deliberately ignored any meaning 'beyond the veil' and concentrated on the simple meaning of the text; while Herder breathed a sigh of relief that this same *Song* was no longer to be 'chopped up for dogma' as though the poet had written it originally for dry scholastic purposes.[1]

Where the seventeenth century, therefore, had begun by preserving the medieval system of prefigurative exegesis of Scripture, the new tendency of the age of enlightenment towards clarity and historicity had stripped the Bible of its allegorical garb and left it visible to all as the literature of an ancient people—divine in its inspirational source but expressed through the lips and in the language of creatures of flesh and blood. Such recognition automatically deprived the classics of the literary monopoly which they had enjoyed during the earlier part of the century. And in the same way as romanticism sought to replace the cold touch of the enlightenment with the warmth of the heart, so the preromantic poets were able to exploit the 'enlightened' unveiling of the scriptures by finding within the biblical text a vivid and passionate literature. Under its still divine auspices, he could free himself from the stylized forms of verse predominant in his day, and forge from his personal experiences poetry which expressed directly and graphically the dictates of his heart rather than of his mind.

[1] J. G. Herder, *Lebensbild* (1846 ed.), i, 464.

3

Nature Refined

No student of the eighteenth century needs to be told that while neo-classical delicacy excluded the term *manure* from poetry, it accepted the circumlocution *stercoraceous heap* as a charming witticism. Fielding and Sterne could depict the boisterous and often bawdy goings-on below stairs, but poetry was for the drawing-room where all must be sedate and formal. In fact, part of the fun involved in imitating the *Georgics* was in demonstrating how much agricultural terminology could be introduced without actually calling a spade a spade. That device of poetic periphrasis learnt from the *Gradus* served to elevate poetry above the 'common' and 'mean', and one unfortunate poetaster who introduced the word *rats* into the opening lines of his poem was laughed to scorn before he could proceed any further. Moreover, once the diction had been refined, the images themselves had to be 'perspicuous' and 'decent'—there was to be no abstruseness of metaphor, no far-fetched comparisons.

Once again, however, the Bible and Homer seemed to have managed very well despite their inattention to these refinements, and from early in the century the discrepancy between neo-classical theory and biblical practice was noted with some concern. Addison, voicing the current perplexity, was perturbed by the incongruous comparison of the Shulamite's nose to a tower of Lebanon, and felt compelled to admit that the biblical authors '. . . very much failed in, or, if you will . . . were very much above the Nicety of the Moderns'.[1] His hesitation in condemning the apparent inappropriateness of the metaphor is itself indicative of the critic's quandary when

[1] *Spectator*, No. 285.

he found a biblical passage contradicting the contemporary rules. Before hinting at a stylistic fault, he had to protect himself against a possible charge of irreverence—a charge of irreverence emanating from his own conscience if not from a hostile reader.

In our own day, when poets and critics feel a closer kinship with the metaphysical school than with the neo-classical, the terms *nicety* and *decency* seem singularly inappropriate as criteria for similes and metaphors, as, indeed, do the terms *common, mean* and *vulgar.* Surrealism has prepared the modern reader for the most incongruous comparisons so that, provided there be some ultimate value to be derived from the comparison, no restrictions are imposed on the range of poetic imagery. But our purpose in this chapter is to enter into the spirit of eighteenth-century criticism, to view biblical imagery from the neo-classical standpoint and by understanding which elements in this imagery offended against prevailing critical views, to observe what resulted from the clash. Since, of all scriptural books, the *Song of Songs* possessed a type of imagery most startlingly opposed to the neo-classical, it would be well to examine it more closely.

(1)

Whether the *Song of Songs* be interpreted as an allegory of God's love for his people, as a collection of epithalamial songs or more simply, as a love-duet, the similes and metaphors must be open to a literal interpretation; for allegory presupposes the validity of the literal as well as the symbolic meaning. Yet, taken literally, the imagery is startling— although startling only in retrospect. At first reading the exotic metaphors, the rich oriental passions create an atmosphere of sensuous delight.

Thou hast ravished my heart, my sister, my spouse; thou hast ravished my heart with one of thy eyes, with one chain of thy neck. How fair is thy love, my sister, my spouse! how much better is thy love than wine! and the smell of thine ointments than all spices! Thy lips, O my spouse, drop as the honeycomb: honey and milk are under thy tongue; and the smell of thy garments is like the smell of Lebanon.

Sight, taste, smell are gratified each in turn and the reader surrenders to the magic spell. It is when one turns back for a second, more dispassionate reading that the strangeness of certain metaphors in the book becomes apparent. The maiden's teeth are compared to a fertile flock of sheep, her neck to an armoury equipped for battle, and her nose to a tower of Lebanon.

In a conceit by Donne—the comparison of love to a pair of compasses, for example—the incongruity of the simile is deliberately cultivated. The reader is momentarily puzzled, but by the resolution of the conceit:

> Thy firmness draws my circle just,
> And makes me end, where I begun,

the basis of comparison has been vividly explained and the metaphor justified. In the *Song*, however, there is no resolution of the incongruity. What is more, the speed with which the images change precludes any elaborate explanation, for the images must be immediate in their effect. The comparison of the maiden's neck to a slender tower—particularly to a tower belonging to King David—is, so far, complimentary. It is the mention of the thousand bucklers, the shields of the mighty hanging there, which makes the image seem strange. And if one attempts a far-fetched interpretation of the shields as beads in her necklace, there are numerous other examples in which the incongruity is even more marked and even less explicable. In the sheep image, for example, why after a vivid and strikingly appropriate simile, is the apparent irrelevancy of fertility introduced?

Thy teeth are like a flock of ewes, all shaped alike, which are come up from the washing; whereof all are paired and none is barren among them.

Or again, how does one connect the final phrase in

Thy two breasts are like two young roes, that are twins, which feed among the lilies.

There was, indeed, a favourite Homeric device, whereby the poet, after drawing a comparison, would become so absorbed in the new image as almost to forget the original, until, after a lengthy passage, he would abruptly recall his reader to the main theme:

And as when a man giveth the hide of a great bull to his folk to stretch, all soaked in fat, and they take and stretch it standing in a circle, and straightway the moisture thereof departeth, and the fat entereth in under the haling of many hands, and it is all stretched throughout—thus they on both sides haled the dead man this way and that.[1]

The colourful details of the image are savoured for their own sake. It is a 'purple passage', attached to the main theme only by the original thread. In the Bible, however, the parallel between the literal and metaphorical sense is normally pursued throughout even the lengthiest of images. The Psalmist, outlining the history of his people since the Exodus, compares them to a vine which in the course of the metaphor never ceases to represent the Hebrews. The comparison stands up to detailed examination at every stage.

Thou didst pluck a vine out of Egypt; thou didst drive out the nations and plant it. Thou didst clear a place before it, and it took deep root and filled the land. The mountains were covered with its shadow, and the mighty cedars with its boughs. She sent out her branches into the sea, and her shoots into the River. Why hast Thou broken down her fences, so that all who pass by the way do pluck her?[2]

The vine symbolizing the Hebrews taking root in their new land is described only insofar as it helps to illustrate the conquest of Canaan; and the function of the metaphor, like that of the verbal form, is subordinated to the explication of the subject-matter. With this in mind, it is all the more difficult to explain the apparently superfluous additions to images in the *Song of Songs*, in which the comparison of the maiden's teeth to the sheep suddenly breaks off at the mention of fertility.

R. G. Moulton has suggested that these various symbols are not intended to be realistic but the very opposite. In his view

[1] *Iliad*, xvii, 389, tr. Lang, Leaf and Myers (London, 1935), p. 318.
[2] Psalm lxxx, 8–13.

they are conventional substitutes for vivid expressions '. . . as widely removed from realistic images as a telegraph code is from onomatopoeia'.[1] Such an explanation, which starts from the assumption that the images are conventional, lacking in realism, is bound to prove unsatisfactory as long as readers continue to be impressed by their very vividness and freshness—for in no other book of the Bible are there any images approaching those of the *Song* in warmth and richness. And, what is more, such a view misses one of the most important elements in the *Song of Songs*—its emotional timbre.

It is abundantly clear that there is within this book a type of imagery far more sensual in quality not merely than that of the rest of the Bible but even than the imagery found in the erotic poetry of most other lands. The effect of the *Song*, with all its frank descriptions of physical delight, is by no means exclusively erotic, yet its appeal is sensual for all that; and I would suggest that we can only explain these images satisfactorily by interpreting them as being drawn not on the visual plane but on the emotional. Of course almost all images are, to a certain extent, dependent upon an emotional comparison, but there is always a visual or intellectual link before the emotional undertones are felt. In T. S. Eliot's image:

> When the evening is spread out against the sky
> Like a patient etherised upon a table,

there are, indeed, deeper emotional associations, such as the fear that life may flicker out; but the main basis of comparison —the pale state of suspended animation—is immediately clear. Yet the comparison of the lover's lips to lilies dripping with honey, or of the maiden's neck to a royal armoury lacks such basic links unless we look for them in the emotion aroused by each of these visions.

The oriental, gazing at the slender tower, perfect not only

---

[1] R. G. Moulton, *The Modern Reader's Bible* (New York, 1907), p. 1448. The same theory was adopted and developed by Israel Baroway in 'The Imagery of Spenser and the *Song of Songs*', *JEGP*, xxxiii (1934).

in the grace of its structure, but also in the fulfilment of its purpose as a defence and stronghold against invasion, would, perhaps, feel the same sense of completeness as when gazing at the neck of his beloved, formed perfectly in every line. As we today might compare a seagull in flight to a Beethoven sonata, relying partly on the similarity of rhythm and harmony, but far more on the effect produced upon our sensations, so the maiden could compare her lover's cheeks to a bed of spices and his lips to lilies dropping with myrrh. For modern readers, conditioned by the illogical sequences of the stream of conscious, such imagery seems only slightly strange; but in its context in the Bible, the rest of which conforms to a more direct form of comparison, the highly emotional quality of the imagery of the *Song* stands out as an isolated phenomenon. It is only by understanding it as an 'emotional' imagery that its peculiar effect can be fully grasped.

(ii)

In the Age of Reason, the detailed analysis of literary effects occupied critics almost as much as in our own day, and it was difficult for the believing Christian to reconcile his reverence for the literary supremacy of the Bible with those literary rules which he so dogmatically asserted elsewhere. The desire for 'perspicuity', for images clearly related to themes, had become a literary criterion, and the flagrant transgression of 'decency' in the *Song of Songs* left the biblical critic nonplussed. But this was not all. It was too glaringly obvious that the Bible resorted to the 'meanest' and, for the neo-classicist, the most inappropriate images to illustrate its sublime themes. It shocked him to find God's destruction of Jerusalem foretold in the words

I will wipe Jerusalem as a man wipeth a dish, wiping it and turning it upside down.[1]

For the most part, he could merely shrug his shoulders and accept biblical standards as being different from his own. But that itself was the first step in acknowledging

---

[1] II Kings xxi, 13.

that neoclassical rules were not exclusively and universally valid.

Joseph Trapp provides an interesting illustration of the dichotomy between standards adopted for biblical criticism and those employed in secular literature. Throughout his lectures he attacks vehemently the absurdity of far-fetched images in poetry, insisting that they should follow the rules of perspicuity and decency. Yet he has nothing but praise for what he inconsistently terms the 'happy boldness' of biblical metaphor which triumphs over '. . . the narrow Rules of mortal Writers'.[1] In effect, then, he demands that human poets adhere strictly to the rigid code of neo-classicism even though he admits that the Bible achieves its superior literary effects by transcending such rules.

This sharp distinction between mortal and sacred writers served partially as a method of excusing differences in literary standards but was, at the same time, symptomatic of a genuine sequestering of biblical literature from literature in general. The critic bared his head before sacred writing, remaining at a respectful distance; and, as we have said, the dichotomy was bound to continue until he felt confident that this divinely inspired literature was capable of standing up to the closest literary scrutiny.

Except for the Bible itself, for which there was already an authorized prose translation, all ancient and foreign literatures which revealed contradictions to the accepted neo-classical rules could be toned down in translation until they conformed. And an examination of the translator's difficulties reveals most clearly the 'transgressions' of the rules which required toning down for the eighteenth-century reader.

Pope's versions of the *Iliad* and *Odyssey* were not so much translations as transmutations. Elijah Fenton, who did much of the hack-work for Pope, was troubled by the cow-heel flung at Ulysses's head. The incident, too important to be omitted, was spoilt by an object too vulgar to be admitted into the refined poetry of the Augustan age. His solution was to describe the cow-heel as

[1] Trapp, *Lectures*, p. 52.

That sinewy fragment . . .
Where to the pastern-bone, by nerves combin'd
The well-horn'd foot indissolubly join'd.[1]

It is significant, however, that when there was no alternative but to admit an image or term distasteful to the neo-classicist because of its common associations, the Bible could be turned to as authority for their inclusion. Pope condescendingly excuses the Homeric metaphors drawn from common life, pointing out that he will admit into his versions '. . . several of those general phrases and manners of expression which have attained veneration even in our language from their use in the Old Testament'.[2] The word *even*, with its implications of the neo-classicist's superiority to the primitive language and literatures of earlier days, reveals the distaste he felt for such common terms even when authorized by the Bible and Homer.

Although the images themselves, when literally translated, offended against contemporary taste, the original classical texts were accepted far more readily. However well acquainted with Latin and Greek the eighteenth-century reader might be, they were still dead languages for him and sufficiently distant for the common associations not to be felt too keenly. When personal tragedy aroused emotions too deep for versification, the neo-classicist turned frequently to Latin in which he felt freer to express his innermost feelings. The patina which time had spread over the Latin language mellowed too vivid a portrayal of emotion, and in much the same way softened the offensiveness of 'vulgar' metaphor. Addison rightly explained that many mean metaphors which would have shocked a Greek or Roman failed to shock his own contemporaries 'because we never hear them pronounced in our streets or in ordinary conversation'.[3] One merely doubts whether they would, in fact, have shocked the Greek or Roman

[1] For an interesting account of further difficulties experienced in translation, see J. Sutherland, *A Preface to Eighteenth Century Poetry* (Oxford, 1950), pp. 88 f., and D. Knight, *Pope and the Heroic Tradition* (New Haven, 1951), chapter i.

[2] Pope, *Preface to the Iliad* (1715).

[3] *Spectator*, No. 285.

whose ear was by no means as delicate as that of his eighteenth-century counterpart.

At any rate, vulgar metaphor and mean terminology were outlawed from neo-classical poetry, and Johnson objected strongly even to the use of so mild a word as *knife* to describe the instrument with which Macbeth commits the murder.

Sentiment is weakened by the name of an instrument used by butchers and cooks in the meanest employments; we do not immediately conceive that any crime of importance is to be committed with a *knife*; or who does not, at last, from long habit of connecting a knife with sordid offices, feel aversion rather than terror?

The poetic diction which he advocated for poetry had to be 'refined from the grossness of domestic use' and we can appreciate Hugh Blair's distaste for the lines in *Henry V*:

And those that leave their valiant bones in France
Dying like men, though buried in your dunghills,
They shall be fam'd; for there the sun shall greet them,
And draw their honours reeking up to heaven.

The very mention of dunghills in poetry was itself offensive to Blair, but the fact that Shakespeare '. . . presently raises a Metaphor from the steam of it' was for him a gross transgression of good taste, revealing in the author an imagination sadly lacking in delicacy.[1] But there were metaphors every bit as startling in the Old Testament, quite apart from the *Song of Songs*, which, unlike those of Shakespeare, could not be condemned on the grounds of indelicacy without danger of offending against religious susceptibilities.

Like most great poets, the biblical prophet turned to the world immediately about him for the images with which to drive home his message, and since his denunciations and demands for penitence were directed for the most part to the masses, to the common people of Israel, the imagery was drawn largely from just those spheres which the neo-classicist condemned as 'mean' and 'common'. In biblical prophecy, which constitutes the main body of biblical poetry, there was

[1] *Rambler*, No. 168, and Hugh Blair, *Lectures on Rhetoric and Belles Lettres* (London, 1783), i, 351.

little room for such philosophical speculations as are to be found, for example, in the book of Job and, as popular oratory, its effect had to be vivid and immediate. Consequently the simple agricultural life of the people was reflected in the poetry of the Bible more than was usual in other countries, where the writing of poetry was usually confined to a small circle of aristocratic intellectuals. In biblical literature, not only were the common people the public to whom such poetry was addressed, but it was largely from their ranks that the poets themselves came. Their humble origin as herdsmen and peasants was an asset to them in the delivery of their message. Unlike a Stephen Duck or a Robert Dodsley, who used his poetic talents to gain an entrée into the upper classes, the biblical prophet renounced what little wealth he possessed and robed himself in a coarse, hairy mantle, either to mingle with the common people to whom his words were addressed or, if at court, as a constant reminder of the divine presence, a man apart and segregated from his regal surroundings. His language, therefore, was the language of the common people. He wrote:

The sin of Judah is written with a pen of iron and with the point of a diamond: it is graven upon the table of their hearts.[1]

and there was nothing to be gained by such periphrasis for *pen* as would have pleased the neo-classicist.

Moreover, where Johnson pleaded for a poetic diction refined from domestic usage, the prophet took not just one word, but complete images from the domestic scene, pursuing them into their smallest details:

They are all adulterers, as an oven heated by the baker, who ceaseth from raising after he hath kneaded the dough, until it be leavened. . . . For they have made ready their heart like an oven, whiles they lie in wait; their baker sleepeth all the night; in the morning it burneth as a flaming fire. They are all hot as an oven. . . . Ephraim is a cake not turned.[2]

Indeed, the Bible often went a good deal further than this in offending against eighteenth-century fastidiousness,

[1] Jeremiah xvii, 1.   [2] Hosea vii, 4–8.

particularly in the frankness with which it discussed matters of physical purity, whether sexual or ritualistic—a frankness which, incidentally, is one of the surest methods of avoiding prurience. The prohibited marital relationships are enumerated in the form 'Thou shalt not uncover the nakedness of . . .' and throughout the early books of the Bible rape, conception, levirate marriage, concubines haggling over the privilege of sleeping with their husband, all these were related simply, directly and without embarrassment. Natural physical desires were acknowledged, their legitimate consummation encouraged, and their abuse condemned. In the poetry of the later books of the Bible it was natural that this theme of marital fidelity should become a favourite illustration of the relationship between God and the Jewish people. The Hebrews were, when faithful, pictured as the untainted bride about to be sanctified in holy matrimony, or (more frequently) when unfaithful, as the prostitute pleading to be taken back by her former husband. It was in the latter connection that the language rose often to the highest level of poetic imagery and, for the neo-classicist, to the lowest degree of indelicacy.

Behold I am against thee, saith the Lord of Hosts; and I will discover thy skirts upon thy face and I will shew the nations thy nakedness, and the kingdoms thy shame. And I will cast abominable filth upon thee, and make thee vile, and set thee as a gazing-stock.[1]

If such was the diction and imagery of the Bible, how was the Augustan to cope with it? Theoretically, he might have ignored such blatant instances of indelicacy, but with Protestantism stemming from the Reformation revolt against a closed Bible, a conspiracy of silence could not be preserved for long, and it was inevitable that some solution should be arrived at.

The line which was eventually taken was closely allied to the primitivist movement. On the principle of *tout comprendre c'est tout pardonner*, a serious attempt was made to understand more fully the background to such images. If it could be shown that the images which shocked by their 'meanness'

[1] Nahum iii, 5.

were, in fact, reflections of activities dignified and respected by the community in which they arose, then the poet was at once acquitted of the charge of 'vulgarity' in verse, and the neo-classical critic could settle back complacently, assured that even the biblical poet wrote according to the rules adopted by the eighteenth century. But the risk involved in such a process was that, by dignifying biblical society, it became idealized. In the same way as primitivism, beginning as scholarly enquiry, ended in profound admiration for the 'noble savage' untainted by civilization, so the attempt to explain away 'mean' images led to a new respect for 'natural' images and the disparagement of artificiality.[1]

In Lowth's lectures, four of which were devoted exclusively to poetic imagery in the Bible, the portrayal of the ancient Hebrews as noble, dignified and wise, as unashamed of their simple but honest tasks, set the tone for his discussion of the imagery. His main point, that images drawn from common life produce greater 'perspicuity', was more an attempt to hitch his advocacy of biblical writings to an accepted contemporary criterion. But in the instances he provided of such imagery he frequently attributed their excellence to the sacredness of the rites from which the metaphors were drawn. This was, of course, an invalid literary criterion, but one calculated to silence adverse criticism and hence to make the poetry more acceptable to eighteenth-century readers. As an extenuation of Ezekiel's image

Woe to the bloody city, to the pot whose scum is therein, and whose scum is not gone out of it.[2]

he reminded the reader that Ezekiel was a priest as well as a prophet; the allusion, therefore, was to the priestly rites, '. . . nor is there a possibility that an image could be accounted mean or disgusting, which was connected with the holy ministration of the Temple'. Apart from the invalidity of the criterion, it is most doubtful whether in fact Ezekiel meant

[1] Cf. T. Lewis, *Origines Hebraeae* (London, 1724), which studied the ancient Hebrews' method of measuring time, their historiography, poetry, sculpture, architecture, weights, measures, coins and so forth.

[2] Ezekiel xxiv, 6.

any more than an ordinary cooking-pot, but the explanation served to present the image in a less 'mean' light, and hence to encourage a more sympathetic approach to other 'common' images in the Bible unconnected with holy rites.

Lowth's approach to the most serious stumbling-block for the neo-classicist, the *Song of Songs*, had important repercussions. For not only did the new treatment of the *Song* inspire Percy's version of it (itself a landmark in Bible translation), but through Herder and others, it won a new respect for the *Song* among the German romantics as an instance of oriental love poetry at its best. In fact, Lowth did very little to solve any fundamental problems, but again it was his infectious admiration which provided his readers with a new approach. His adoption of Bossuet's theory that the *Song* was an epithalamial poem which could be divided into seven sections to correspond with the traditional seven-day celebration of Hebrew weddings, brought to the fore the picture of the Hebrews in their idyllic setting. But where even so perceptive a critic as Addison had mocked, as far as he dared, at the comparison of a nose to the tower of Lebanon, Lowth admired the identification with '. . . some turret of the citadel of Sion, more lofty than the rest, remarkable for its elegance, and not less illustrious for its architecture'. Presented in that way, the simile ceased to shock. The method was emotive rather than critical but the staunch neo-classicists in his audience could now begin to think that the exotic and apparently wild imagery of the *Song* was, in the final analysis, not alien to Reason. With his resistance broken—and it was largely by the emphasis on the sacredness of Zion that it was broken—he could turn to it as true poetry, worthy of imitation.

Once the neo-classicist did approach the Bible with a respect for its literary merits, one of the first points to strike him about its imagery was its 'perspicuity'. In contrast to the periphrases of Latin verse which had been imported so liberally into the verse of the eighteenth century, it was largely by a process of condensation, by swift changes of simple, direct images that the Bible achieved its effect, and this simplicity was true of diction as well as metaphor. Of the innumerable instances in which the Bible mentions the sky, not once is it referred to as anything even vaguely like *the blue vault of heaven* which Kames recommended. It is always *the heavens* simply and directly, and even when the Psalmist is at pains to emphasize the magnificence of its testimony to God, he says unaffectedly:

> The heavens relate the glory of the Lord.

In Addison's version, the sentiment becomes:

> The Spacious Firmament on High
> With all the blue Etherial Sky
> And spangled Heavens, a Shining Frame,
> Their great Original proclaim.[1]

By expansion and diffusion he has transformed the verse into something essentially different, and in clothing the nakedness of biblical diction Addison has obscured one of its greatest virtues. The new admiration for the simplicity of biblical diction was, like the new respect for images drawn from common, domestic scenes and from nature rather than mythology, an important step towards the Wordsworthian concept of poetry.

But apart from the subject-matter of the imagery, there was in texture and presentation a vast difference between the neo-classical and the biblical. One of Pope's most powerful passages depicts the triumph of Chaos:

> As one by one at dread Medea's strain,
> The sick'ning stars fade off the etherial plain;
> As Argus's eyes, by Hermes' wand opprest,
> Clos'd one by one to everlasting rest;
> Thus at her felt approach and secret might
> Art after Art goes out and all is Night.[2]

Each simile drops ponderously into position, relished for its own sake, yet building up towards the power of the last line. In contrast the biblical effect is achieved by a series of swift, rapier-like thrusts, each exactly on the mark, each independent, yet each subordinated to the central idea of God's

---

[1] *Spectator*, No. 465. [2] Pope, *Dunciad*, iv, 635.

immense power, which is, of course, responsible even for the
fire, the wind, and the flame.

> As the stubble before the wind:
> As the fire which burneth the forest,
> As the flame which kindleth the mountains;
> So do Thou pursue them with Thy tempests,
> And with Thy whirlwind make them afraid.[1]

Its emotional impact is immediate, where Pope tends to build
up by slow accumulation an ultimately crushing anger or contempt; and again the biblical form has a greater kinship with
the romantic. Pope, of course, cultivated colloquialisms and
played down periphrases in his Horatian satires and epistles,
but he would never do so in the epic or any elevated genre.
And if the circumlocutions are less frequent in such later poets
as Dyer, Shenstone and Akenside, their verse is still heavy
with epithets which blunt any innate sharpness of vision. In
Dyer's *Grongar Hill*, despite its response to the beauties of the
natural world, the Latinate syntactic involutions and epi-
thetizing almost smother the freshness of the vision.

> Silent Nymph, with curious Eye!
> Who, the purple Ev'ning, lye
> On the Mountain's lonely Van,
> Beyond the Noise of busy Man,
> Painting fair the form of Things,
> While the yellow Linnet sings;
> Or the tuneful Nightingale
> Charms the Forest with her Tale;
> Come with all thy various Hues,
> Come, and aid thy sister Muse.

As the century moved on, brevity, simplicity and emotional directness replaced the more cumbersome periphrases of
neo-classical verse. In his *Olney Hymns*, fashioned from biblical subject-matter, Cowper wrote with a simplicity of diction
and imagery startlingly different from the Latinate phraseology which he employed in most of his secular poems:

> I want that grace that springs from thee,
> That quickens all things where it flows,
> And makes a wretched thorn like me
> Bloom as the myrtle or the rose.[2]

[1] Psalm lxxxiii, 14.　　　　　　　　[2] Cowper, *Olney Hymn*, liv.

In one of his lengthy secular poems he expresses almost the identical thought in conventional neo-classical terms, providing us with a perfect instance of the effects produced by the old and new techniques:

> Man's heart had been impenetrably sealed,
> Like theirs that cleave the flood or graze the field,
> Had not his Maker's all-bestowing hand
> Given him a soul and bade him understand.[1]

The difference in tone is enormous. The intensely personal *I* and *thee* of the former is expressed here in terms of *man's heart* and *his Maker's all-bestowing hand* and the rhetorical second line means no more than 'like fish or sheep'; but Cowper feels instinctively that the diction must be elevated to the level of poetry. Yet when he works closely with the Bible and under its aegis attempts to capture the devotional humility of the Psalmist, he chooses, again instinctively, the directness of biblical language.

Blake, of course, drew his store of images straight from the Scriptures, borrowing with them the moral connotations which they had borne there. The innocent lambs of the Psalmist, the fruitful vine under which the ancient Hebrew rested, the deceitful serpent of Genesis, the angels of good tidings and even the harlots symbolic of Israel's shame and infidelity are woven into the tapestry of his *Songs of Innocence and Experience* without a trace of embarrassment or apology. Each image is introduced simply, without stylistic embellishment and, for that very reason, with magical effect.

> Like a serpent in the day
> Underneath my vines he lay:
> Like a serpent in the night
> He embraced my myrtle bright.[2]

One can almost hear an Augustan poet solemnly replacing that vivid *embraced* with

> For want of arms, wrapped round his gleaming coils.

The preromantic, seeking a less cumbersome poetic technique, used the Bible sometimes unconsciously as a source of

---

[1] Cowper, *Conversation*, 427 f.   [2] Blake, *Infant Sorrow*, 29.

fresh and lively imagery. The biblical background of Smart and Blake is patent in the imagery, idiom and rhythms. By the time of Wordsworth, the same directness and simplicity is there but the biblical source is no longer apparent. In one of his best known poems, Wordsworth describes Lucy with extraordinary vividness as

> A violet by a mossy stone
> Half hidden from the eye!
> Fair as a star, when only one
> Is shining in the sky.

There is here no trace of Augustan periphrasis, nor of poetic diction and, were it not for Wordsworth's own testimony to the biblical source, it would be difficult to argue that this simplicity of imagery and language was influenced by the biblical forms. For at this stage there is no biblical association to confirm the scriptural debt.

However, in Wordsworth's famous attack upon poetic diction which prefaced the *Lyrical Ballads*—the first formulation of the romantic break with neo-classical diction—there appears the following passage:

Perhaps in no way, by positive example, could more easily be given a notion of what I mean by the phrase poetic diction than by referring to a comparison between the metrical paraphrase which we have of passages as they exist in the Old and New Testament, and those passages as they exist in our common Translation.

And as illustration he quotes in full Johnson's paraphrase of some verses from Proverbs vi.

> Turn on the prudent Ant thy heedless eyes,
> Observe her labours, Sluggard, and be wise;
> No stern command, no monitory voice,
> Prescribes her duties, or directs her choice;
> Yet timely provident, she hastes away
> To snatch the blessings of a plenteous day;
> When fruitful Summer loads the teeming plain,
> She crops the harvest, and she stores the grain.
> How long shall sloth usurp thy useless hours,
> Unnerve thy vigour, and enchain thy powers?
> While artful shades thy downy couch enclose,
> And soft solicitation courts repose,

Amidst the drowsy charms of dull delight,
Year chases year with unremitted flight,
Till Want now following, fraudulent and slow,
Shall spring to seize thee like an ambush'd foe.

In contrast he quotes, again in full, the original verses, so that what he terms the 'hubbub of words' in Johnson should be apparent to the reader.

Go to the Ant, thou Sluggard, consider her ways, and be wise: which having no guide, overseer, or ruler, provideth her meat in the summer, and gathereth her food in the harvest. How long wilt thou sleep, O Sluggard? when wilt thou arise out of thy sleep? Yet a little sleep, a little slumber, a little folding of the hands to sleep. So shall thy poverty come as one that travelleth, and thy want as an armed man.

For Wordsworth, then, the Bible offered the clearest example of poetry free from artificiality of diction, while the 'poetic' paraphrases whereby the neo-classicist had hoped to elevate the biblical language Wordsworth rejected as perversions of the original. And in this document central to the formulation of romantic poetry, he holds up the Bible to the reader as the kind of poetry he wishes could be introduced for the new age.

At this point we should recall that the natural imagery of the Bible might never have been taken as a model if critics and poets had not come to recognize prose translations of the Scriptures as poetic in themselves. This recognition, in turn, could not have occurred without the theory of parallelism which showed that the biblical rhythm of thought could only be preserved in a literal translation, and that it was almost completely destroyed if transmuted into neo-classical verse-forms. Through the curtain of Augustan paraphrase, the simplicity of biblical imagery and diction was obscured beyond recognition. Only with the removal of that curtain could it contribute to the transition from the generalizing epithets and witty periphrases of Queen Anne's day to the vivid directness of Blake and Wordsworth.

4

Patriarchal Nobility

Behind the neo-classicist's search for ultimate criteria of literary excellence lay the conviction that all men were fundamentally alike, that Reason was the supreme touchstone, and that therefore the standards of taste established by Reason would be acceptable to the entire civilized world. The very fact that 'taste' to the eighteenth-century critic meant, not individual preference, but that which was agreed upon by the majority, presupposed this sense of universal concord. The ideal work of art was one

> . . . by no particular taste confin'd
> Whose universal pattern strikes the mind[1]

and the neo-classicist erroneously assumed that this universal pattern was identical with the particular taste of his own age.

It was, indeed, the rising interest in the 'natural effusions' of the primitives and the colourful passions of oriental literature which eventually broke down this static concept by championing literary works which transgressed the accepted rules. But to champion such writings in an age deliberately excluding from society the exotic, the eccentric and the strange was to invite scorn and derision. Among the various primitive and oriental writings, one work alone could never be sneered at as barbarous, however incongruous its imagery and stylistic techniques might appear. For the Bible was, after all, a holy work, and while Homer could be castigated for his lapses from good taste, the divine origin of the Scriptures and the availability of a literal authorized translation ensured that their

[1] Thomas Warton, *Verses on Reynold's Window*, 65–6.

78

natural vigour and passion could be neither concealed nor condemned. Instinctively, the eighteenth-century innovator used the Bible time after time as a shield against derision and, indeed, as justification for this new admiration of unsophisticated writings. Addison's praise for the artless splendour of *Chevy Chace* was dismissed contemptuously as the quirk of an otherwise impeccable critic, but his essentially similar admiration for the ardour and simplicity of the Psalter not only went unchallenged but was greeted with warm approval.[1]

The story of the Noble Savage in literature, typified by the American Indian, the Tahitian and such fictional figures as Oroonoko, has been amply told.[2] But it must be distinguished from that aspect of primitivism which concerns us here. For the Noble Savage himself, of whom Oroonoko and Crusoe's Man Friday may serve as examples, was a symptom of the European's sense of superiority. True, in his yearning for the Golden Age, the European tended to idealize that purity and simplicity which the savage had retained at the expense of his mental and cultural advancement. However, the reader never doubts that, if Friday has succeeded in paring down the doctrinal superfluities of Crusoe's Christianity, he has made the better bargain by being introduced to Christianity at all, and we are supposed to be constantly surprised at the degree of loyalty and native intelligence in one not bred on eighteenth-century culture.

The second form of primitivism is in a sense an offspring of the Noble Savage interest which existed in the eighteenth century side by side with its parent. For if the former arose from a sense of condescension on the part of the eighteenth-century writer, the latter betokened a deep admiration. Here the primitive has achieved the wholesomeness of a fully developed and often superior culture without being corrupted, like the Augustan Age, by the evils of urban civilization. Among

---

[1] *Spectator*, Nos. 70 and 489. For an account of the reception accorded to the *Chevy Chace* essay, see R. P. McCutcheon, 'Another Burlesque of Addison's Ballad Criticism', *SP*, xxiii (1926), 451, and S. B. Hustvedt, *Ballad Criticism . . . during the Eighteenth Century* (New York, 1916), pp. 65–78.

[2] H. N. Fairchild, *The Noble Savage* (New York, 1928).

the Greeks, Homer is singled out as depicting a society essentially simple in structure and morality, yet highly intelligent
and admirable. The Chinese, exemplifying the parallel oriental
movement, are seen as possessing a greater stock of wisdom,
and a more developed architecture and gardening technique.
And the Hebrew patriarchs, distinguished by a purer religion
than that of contemporary England (considering, of course,
that they pre-dated the Christian Messiah) wrote poetry closer
to the source of divine inspiration and more naturally expres-
sive of the unveiled feelings of the poet than the sophisticated
verses of Hanoverian England. It is this admiration for
primitivist literature that interests us here.

The growth and development of this primitivism is too
well known to require more than brief summary. The earliest
recognition of the difference in literary standards between one
country and another had its source in the theory that climate
affected character and hence poetic style. In the same way as
humidity and heat in the body had, through the seventeenth-
century theory of the humours, been held responsible for
affecting man's temper and character, so variations in climate
were held accountable for the characteristics of national
literatures. It was noted that 'As in Physic, so in Poetry, there
must be a regard had to the Clime, Nature and Customs of the
People',[1] but at this stage the climatic factor was quoted more
as an extenuation than as a plea for better understanding.
Oriental culture, frequently exaggerated by the lurid tales
brought back from the East, was too colourful and passionate
for the late seventeenth century, and Rymer complained im-
patiently of the 'wild, vast and unbridled' fancy of the Arabians
which produced monstrous conceptions lacking all exactness
and proportion.[2]

At the turn of the century, however, when the dislike of
enthusiasm was less violent, the *Arabian Nights*, translated
into French by Galland, became known in England and
interest in the East increased. At the same time, the new

---

[1] C. Gildon, *Vindication of Cowley and Waller* (1694), in W. H.
Durham, *Critical Essays of the Eighteenth Century* (London, 1915), p. 4.

[2] T. Rymer, *Preface to Rapin* (1674) in Spingarn, ii, 165.

allowances made for the oppressive heat of Arabia led Steele to wonder what literary effects the icy blasts of the North might produce, and he published in 1712 a translation of a Lapland love song, noting (perhaps with his tongue in his cheek) the astonishing warmth of emotion which was yet to be found in so cold a climate.[1]

The antiquarian interest in primitive writing and the scholarly research into foreign literatures began in much the same way as an archaeologist examines an ancient weapon. His admiration for craftsmanship exhibited under such difficult conditions is tinged with an air of condescension towards an age which had not yet discovered gunpowder. But the very contact with these literatures, however academic its original intent, led eventually to a reassessment of neo-classical standards, and the realization that it was a mistake to imagine a Platonic ideal for literature of which the eighteenth century had the closest copy. Pope, it is true, had enunciated the dictum of 'relativism', that a historical and geographical perspective was essential to criticism:

> Know well each ancient's proper character,
> His fable, subject, scope in every page,
> Religion, country, genius of his age.
> Without all these at once before your eyes,
> Cavil you may, but never criticise.

but he would have been surprised to find this critical principle carried literally into practice. It was not so much a call for a deeper understanding of the ancients as a warning to know one's facts before embarking on criticism. A few years later he showed a greater awareness of the necessity for this sense of perspective when he declared that to judge Shakespeare by Aristotle's rules was like '. . . trying a man by the Laws of one country who acted under those of another',[2] but he implied

---

[1] *Spectator*, No. 366. See also S. C. Chew, *The Crescent and the Rose* (New York, 1937), which examines seventeenth-century interest in the East. M. P. Conant, *The Oriental Tale in England in the Eighteenth Century* (New York, 1908), and E. Osborne, *Oriental Diction and Theme in English Verse, 1740–1840*, both specifically exclude biblical orientalism from their studies.

[2] Pope, *Preface to Shakespeare* (1725).

that it was a pity Shakespeare did not act under the laws of a rather more civilized country.

The first clear sign (outside biblical criticism) of a serious attempt to view the ancients in perspective was Blackwell's *Enquiry into the Life and Writings of Homer* (1735), which, as the title suggests, tried to view the Homeric poems in the light of the surroundings in which the poet had lived. His main thesis, and a valid one, was that a poem depends upon the manners of the age in which it is produced and that it was therefore ridiculous to imitate the Homeric epic in the eighteenth century. His warning might at first sight appear to militate against the growing desire to look to the ancient past for poetic models; but in fact, the call for poetry based on the poet's first-hand experiences as opposed to the conventional classical imitations encouraged an investigation of the way in which poets of other lands and periods had used their own environments in their imagery, and it resulted in the application of those same methods to contemporary verse. Blackwell's own work was intended to afford an example of such an investigation, and his suggestions were carried to an exaggerated degree by Robert Wood, who journeyed to the site of Troy in order to recite the *Iliad* in its true setting.[1]

This 'relativist' theory, developed in such works as J. Harris's *Hermes* (1751), reached its culmination in Hurd's *Letters on Chivalry* (1762) which translated the literary controversy into architectural terms. Both Greek and Gothic architecture, he pointed out, appeared deformed when judged by each other's rules; yet they were both admirable styles when viewed according to the artistic standards of their own eras. Similarly, therefore, any attempt to establish a universal set of literary criteria was doomed to failure. With this essential point made, the two movements of primitivism and orientalism could develop more freely, leading on the one hand to Percy's *Reliques of Antient English Poetry* (1765) and the spate of similar ballad collections, and on the other to Sir William Jones's *Essay on the Poetry of the Eastern Nations* (1772).

[1] R. Wood, *An Essay on the Original Genius of Homer* (London, 1769).

Such, in brief résumé, was the growth of these two movements. But these very relativist views are to be found much earlier in the realm of biblical criticism. Indeed, if 'relativism' blossomed in the revival of the secular ballad and the cult of an exotic Arabianism, its seeds (as a comparison of the dates confirms) had been nurtured in the soil of biblical criticism.

To give but one instance, Pope himself suddenly expressed a perfectly serious desire to write 'a Persian fable; in which I should have given a full loose to description and imagination. It would have been a very wild thing if I had executed it.'[1] The picture of an eminently sober Pope writing a 'very wild' poem is certainly intriguing, but a letter he received from Lady Mary Wortley Montagu shows the source of this sudden eccentricity to be the Bible itself. In Adrianople, she had heard that Ibrahim Pasha, the reigning favourite, had either written or commissioned some verses to his bride, which Lady Mary regarded as 'most wonderfully resembling the Song of Solomon'. She took great pains to translate them literally, and sent the result to Pope, pointing out the supposed similarity. The verses begin:

> The nightingale now wanders in the vines:
> Her passion is to seek roses;
> I went down to admire the beauty of the vines.
> The sweetness of your charms has ravished my soul.
> Your eyes are black and lovely,
> But wild and disdainful as those of the stag.[2]

There is indeed some similarity to the imagery of the *Song of Songs*, but what concerns us more closely is that for Pope the sole justification—and a sufficient justification—for indulging in exotic orientalism was this scriptural authority.

The voluptuous and exotic images of the *Song of Songs*, the lustful and illicit loves of David and Amnon, the scenes of luxuriant grapevines and pomegranates, all evoked the colourful picture of the Orient which earlier travellers had established in the minds of Englishmen; while on the other

[1] J. Spence, *Anecdotes*, ed. S. W. Singer (London, 1820), p. 140.
[2] Lady Mary Wortley Montagu, *Letters and Works*, ed. W. Moy Thomas (London, 1893), i, 304.

hand the pastoral simplicity of Ruth amid the alien corn and of young David guarding the flocks of Jesse were readily associated with the dignity of the ancient past before the corruption and complexities of 'civilization'. The Bible was ideally suited to the movements both of primitivism and of orientalism, and although biblical exegesis in the seventeenth century was primarily concerned with the comparatively new problem of examining the literal meaning of the text, and of elucidating the religious and moral significance of the ancient stories, this very research into the historical background produced a new attraction for the way of life it revealed.

The central problem in the seventeenth-century literary assessment of the Bible was, as we have seen, that the critic was unsure whether he was discussing verse or prose and, if verse, he did not understand the nature of its structure. In addition, his unfamiliarity with the rites and customs of the ancient Hebrews acted as an obstacle to a full understanding of their literature. Boyle complained that the exact meaning of various Hebrew words and phrases had been lost, and hence that it was impossible to verify '. . . a multitude of particulars relating to the Topography, History, Rites, Opinions, Factions, Customs, etc., of the ancient Jews and Neighbouring Nations'.[1] Despite the sociological presentation of the problem, his prime interest was its literary effects; for he was rather like a Victorian moralist trying to appreciate the story of Launcelot and Guinevere with no knowledge of the courtly love tradition. He responded to the story's literary power, but felt that he was missing some essential clues which would deepen and broaden its significance.

This scholarly interest in the oriental setting of the Bible continued to grow, and a work published in 1724 made a study of '. . . the Method of measuring Time among the Hebrews, their Learning . . . their Historiography, Poetry, Printing, Sculpture, Architecture; their Weights, Measures and Coins etc.'[2] It was intended for the elucidation of textual difficulties rather than for a profounder understanding of ancient Hebrew

[1] Boyle, op. cit., p. 14.
[2] Thomas Lewis, *Origines Hebraeae* (London, 1724).

culture, but it was a symptom of this wider desire to become acquainted with the ancient Hebrews, to visualize them in their natural setting and hence to reinterpret their literature from a more sympathetic standpoint.

An interesting sidelight on the Bible as primitivist literature is the view held at that time that Hebrew was the language spoken in Eden, and therefore the most 'primitive' of all languages. It is in periods of excessive sophistication that man turns longingly towards idyllic scenes of simplicity and primeval innocence, and away from the corruptions of civilization. In the effete society of later Greece, Theocritus created the idyll, to be copied later in the pastoral poems of Augustan Rome. If the eighteenth century yearned for simplicity, the pastoral, now heavily stylized by its classical associations, could no longer satisfy it, and what better model of primeval innocence could be found than Eden before the Fall, with which setting the language of the Bible was associated? Aaron Hill maintained that God '. . . taught poetry first to the Hebrews and the Hebrews to mankind in general',[1] and there were frequent references to the 'natural' language of the Hebrews based upon the idea that theirs was the original tongue.

An anonymous work entitled, like Hill's, *Creation* (1750) developed this linguistic theory into a semantic study of Hebrew in which the biblical description of Adam busily inventing 'natural' names for all the animals formed the basis for a new conception of the language. In effect, here was the first recognition that the greater tangibility of Hebrew writing had its source in the basic triliteral roots. Yet even more significant was the implication that such naturalism was a distinct advantage over the sophistication of contemporary literature. And Parkhurst, the leading Hebrew lexicographer of the age, made this implication explicit by claiming that because of its peculiar semantic origins, the Hebrew language

[1] A. Hill, *Preface to 'Creation'* (1720), ed. G. G. Pahl (London, 1949). Robert Dodsley made strange use of biblical primitivism in his publication under the pseudonym Nathan ben Saddi of *The Chronicles of the Kings of England Written in the Manner of the Ancient Jewish Historians* (London, 1740), which ran to four editions.

was '. . . the most easy and natural of any that was ever spoken in the world'.[1]

Cowper, on the assumption that Hebrew was spoken in Eden, visualized Adam composing poems in a language admirably suited to the simple piety of its divine theme, and he yearned for those far-off days when poetry was spontaneous, ecstatic, and free from artistic 'form'—the three main distinctions between neo-classicism and romanticism.

> . . . ere yet innocence of heart
> Had faded, poetry was not an art;
> Language above all teaching, or, if taught,
> Only by gratitude and glowing thought,
> Elegant as simplicity and warm
> As ecstasy unmanacled by form,
> Not prompted, as in our degenerate days,
> By low ambition and the thirst of praise,
> Was natural as is the flowing stream,
> And yet magnificent—a God the theme.[2]

But this whimsical interest in the Hebrew of Eden played only a minor part in the primitivist movement. A more serious contribution was John Husbands' preface to *A Miscellany of Poems* (1731) which did much to further the new view of the Bible as a primitive, oriental literature. In this preface Husbands contrasted the classics on the one hand with a group consisting of the Bible, Lapland songs, Runic and Welsh odes on the other. His statement that he did not remember to have seen the subject handled *ex professo* by anyone lacked substance, but the new direction which he gave to the theory was important.

He dismissed as impracticable any attempt to reduce Hebrew to metrical form, but he did recognize the oriental splendour of biblical writing and was prepared to judge it by its own standards. 'How ridiculous', he cried, 'would those pompous titles given to the Ottoman Emperors sound among us: God on Earth, Shadow of God, Sole Monarch of the World,

---

[1] This appears only in the 1762 edition. A new preface was written in 1778.

[2] Cowper, *Table Talk*, 583 f.

Brother of the Sun and Moon?'[1] and he marvelled at the description of the dawn in Job as the 'eyelids of the morning'.

Similarly, Lowth's conception of the ancient Hebrews as a nation of husbandmen and shepherds whose heroes, kings and prophets were called from the plough and from the stall expressed itself most effectively not so much in the few scattered references to their simplicity as in his explanation of metaphors, allegories, and anthropomorphisms in the light of the primitive agricultural setting. *Covering thyself with light as with a garment,* he traces to its source in the white sacerdotal robes, and *scattering thine enemy like chaff* to the particular method of threshing; and this defence of supposedly 'mean' metaphor could never have been effective if his feelings towards these 'husbandmen' had been tinged with condescension. They were, he maintained, a people superior in dignity to his own contemporaries and poorer only in the luxury, levity and pride of artificial civilization.

Particularly significant is that, whereas Hurd's famous remarks on Gothic architecture appeared in 1762, Lowth's enunciation of relativism in terms far more vigorous had taken place nearly twenty years before. Hurd's comments are rightly regarded as the earliest forthright statement of literary relativism since he proceeded to discuss in the light of it such ancient works as the *Faerie Queene*. But Lowth, in the narrower sphere of biblical appreciation had gone even further. Merely to make allowance for discrepancies in taste was, he insisted, insufficient. 'We must see all things with their eyes, estimate all things by their opinions; and we must endeavour as much a possible to read Hebrew as the Hebrews would have read it.' He concluded by comparing the ideal critic to an astronomer who conceives himself as migrating from planet to planet in order to survey the universe from different vantage points, each as valid as its neighbour's, and thereby he rejected out of hand the superiority of neo-classical criteria.[2]

The new portrayal of the simple dignity of the ancient

[1] Cf. R. S. Crane, 'An Early Enthusiast for Primitive Poetry', *MLN*, xxxvii (1922), 27.
[2] *Lectures*, v and vii.

Hebrews found expression a few years later in Goldsmith's *Oratorio* (1764) on the enslavement of the Jews in Babylon. With echoes of the Psalm 'By the waters of Babylon . . .', the prophets are depicted as courageous and dignified patriarchal figures, despising the ribald merriment of their barbarous captors, who are attempting to force them to sing songs of Zion. The First Prophet comforts his people:

> Ye captive tribes, that hourly work and weep
> Where flows Euphrates murmuring to the deep,
> Suspend your woes awhile, the task suspend,
> And turn to God, your father and your friend.
> Insulted, chained, and all the world our foe,
> Our God alone is all we boast below.

The source of this sympathetic description is a new sense of identification with the ancient Hebrews which played no small part in the enormous popularity of the Handelian oratorio itself. Milton's ability to see in himself a reflection of the biblical Samson was a residue of the sixteenth-century Protestant's insistence upon the biblical Covenant of which he believed himself to be the heir. But this sympathy had been replaced by the cynicism of Dryden's *Absalom and Achitophel* with its amused contempt for the Pharisees:

> The Jews, a headstrong, moody, murm'ring race,
> As ever tried th' extent and stretch of grace;
> God's pampered people, whom, debauch'd with ease,
> No king could govern, nor no God could please.

However, the rising middle class of the new industrial era had inherited from the Puritans, together with other qualities, their sense of identification with the Old Testament heroes, and the advocates of biblical primitivism found an eager audience in this increasingly numerous group. Most of the Handelian oratorios were devoted to Old Testament themes in which Judas Maccabaeus's overthrow of a foreign tyrant or Joshua's conquest of the Promised Land merged almost imperceptibly with the intense patriotism of the English people as they rose on the wave of imperial expansion, convinced that they were carrying the true word of God to the pagan corners of the earth. As a British audience heard the words

While lawless tyrants, with ambition blind,
Mock solemn faith, waste worlds, and thin mankind,
Israel can boast a leader just and brave,
A friend to freedom and ordained to save.
   Thus bless'd to heaven your voices raise
   In songs of thanks and hymns of praise.

they were thinking less of Joshua and his army than of their own intrepid spirit of adventure, their love of justice, and their sincere, if somewhat vague, religious aspirations.

Therefore, although today the artistic value of these oratorios lies almost exclusively in the musical score, the importance of the libretto for contemporary audiences should not be underestimated. The subtitle *An Oratorio, or Sacred Drama*, was intended to remind the audience that the work consisted of a biblical drama set to music rather than a musical concert which happened to use a biblical theme. The latter would have dissuaded many upright citizens from attending, and the performance in a Town Hall rather than an opera house was intended to conciliate the more scrupulous. Unlike the imported Italian opera, its English text was intelligible to all. Indeed, Handel's ability to compose a score whose solemnity and majesty did not fall short of his sacred text was soon recognized as his greatest asset, and the audience watched carefully for the harmonious synthesis of the two. This contemporary concern with the texts themselves makes it clear that the peculiarly English phenomenon, the oratorio, formed a significant part of the biblical primitivist movement in which the eighteenth-century Englishman saw himself in terms of the martial heroes of the Scriptures, fighting their wars or enduring their captivity with that simple dignity now associated with the ancient past.

In the same year as Goldsmith's oratorio was published, there appeared the translation of the *Song of Solomon* by Bishop Percy. It appeared only one year before the *Reliques*, yet the difference in presentation between the two works is remarkable, and throws considerable light on the position of the Bible in the primitivist movement. In the preface to his biblical translation, Percy made particular mention of the antiquity of the work, the differences in climatic conditions between Palestine and England, and the disparity in manners, taste, and standards of excellence—but all this without a hint of apology for the Hebrews. On the contrary, he implies that they were at the very least the equal of the eighteenth-century reader, and by their greater simplicity and naturalness, in many ways his superior.

However, when a year later he introduced his *Reliques*, he hastened to assure the reader that this collection had served merely as 'a relaxation from graver studies'. After so many years of interest in primitive poetry, some half-century after Addison's championing of *Chevy Chace*, the leading protagonist of the ballads still felt it necessary to apologize for them as '. . . the barbarous productions of an unpolished age', and he sheltered behind preceding primitivists who, he hoped, would serve 'as an amulet to guard him from every unfavourable censure for having bestowed any attention on a parcel of Old Ballads'. Moreover, his extensive tampering with the text of the ballads in an attempt to make them conformable to contemporary taste shows his own qualms about their literary merit. Where the Bible had by this time been accepted as the literature of an ancient, oriental people free from the trammels of so-called civilization, and hence as a worthy example of primitivist literature, the ballads were only being cautiously introduced to the reader. The ridicule with which they were greeted included, we may recall, his friend Dr. Johnson's parody:

> I put my hat upon my head
> And walked into the Strand,
> And there I met another man
> Whose hat was in his hand.

Not least significant is the fact that Percy's biblical translation preceded the publication of the *Reliques*. Like the latter, it aimed at rescuing an ancient poem from obscurity (that of allegorizing commentators) and in the task of revalidating ancient writing he instinctively turned first to the Bible, as though aware that no violent antagonism would be aroused by such holy work.

As oriental literature, the Bible was not only appreciated ahead of the general movement but, as has been insufficiently recognized, was largely the source for the most important orientalist works of the century. Apart from the imitations of the *Arabian Nights*, the most significant publication advocating oriental literature previous to that of Sir William Jones was by Thomas Harmer, each of whose books was concerned primarily with the Bible. The main theme of the first, *Observations on Divers Passages of Scripture* (1764), was that the Bible was written in an oriental country, and that only by comparing incidents from the Scriptures with the folk-lore, customs, and attitudes of the surrounding countries could an accurate picture of the biblical scene be obtained. It was this identification of Palestine with its geographical, and therefore cultural, location which was the specific contribution of the book, and it laid a foundation for further oriental studies. Once again, the overt purpose of the book was to assist textual exegesis, but the incidental attempt to understand an oriental culture, as it were from within, demanded from the reader a temporary suspension of eighteenth-century standards, a suspension which weakened their authority when they were resumed.

Harmer's second work, published like the first anonymously, was entitled *The Outlines of a New Commentary on Solomon's Song Drawn by the Help of Instruction from the East* (1768), and, as its title indicates, it emphasized once more the oriental qualities of the Bible with specific reference to its most exotic book. It was largely a friendly criticism of Percy's translation, but it delved more deeply into the oriental aspects of the work, noting, for example, Lady Mary Wortley Montagu's comparison of a Turkish love-poem to the *Song*. But where Lady Mary's comparison had been intended as a justification of the oriental poem on the grounds of its biblical qualities, Harmer now reversed the process to offer the Turkish poem as 'proof' of the orientalism of the Scriptures. The allegorical interpretation of the *Song* which had occupied medieval and, indeed, even seventeenth-century scholars almost to the exclusion of any literary appreciation was now forgotten, and the

91

poem, as an Eastern love-song, was examined solely for its literary merits.

Sir William Jones's influential *Essay on the Poetry of the Eastern Nations* (1772) portrayed the orientals in much the same way as Goldsmith had portrayed the ancient Hebrews. They quietly watch their flocks and camels as they sing their native songs '. . . which they pour out ex tempore, professing a contempt for the stately pillars and solemn buildings of cities, compared with the natural charms of the country and the coolness of their tents'.[1] There is the same contempt for civilization; and the admiring description of their extemporaneous outpourings of song marks a significant move towards the romantic conception of poetry as the 'spontaneous overflow of powerful feeling'. However, Jones assured his readers that they would not find oriental literature strange, on the grounds that its qualities were similar to those of the Bible which had already won literary recognition;[2] and the profound admiration with which he mentions Lowth leaves no doubt of his own acquaintance with those writings on biblical primitivism which had laid the foundations for his own championing of orientalism.

The primitivism of the romantics themselves drew its inspiration less from the Bible than from the revival of interest in the ballads. But the ballad movement itself had been fostered by the Bible. As we have seen from the dates, Addison shocked his readers by admiring the simplicity of *Chevy Chace* at a time when his admiration of biblical primitivism went unchallenged. Hill's preface to *Creation* (1720) and Husbands' preface to his *Miscellany* (1731) advocated the simplicity and artlessness of scriptural literature before even so early a primitivist work as Blackwell's *Enquiry* (1735) into Homer's life, and Lowth's insistence upon historical relativism couched in terms far more forceful than Hurd's, forestalled the latter by some twenty years. Moreover, the translation of the *Song of Songs* by Percy, published the year previous to

[1] Sir William Jones, *Works*, ed. A. M. Jones (London, 1799), iv, 532.
[2] *Traité sur la Poésie Orientale* (which is not a translation of the Essay) in *Works*, ed. cit., v, 446. For Lowth references see *Works*, ii, 417 and 483.

his timorous presentation of the *Reliques*, reveals in its enthusiastic preface how far the ballad movement lagged behind the growing admiration for biblical primitivism. And this primitivist interest in the *Song of Songs* was itself linked with orientalism so that the leading orientalists of the country, Thomas Harmer and Sir William Jones, acknowledged their debt to the Bible and indeed modelled much of their own work on the oriental interests of the new biblical critics.

Not only in England, but on the continent too the *Song of Songs* had won admiration as a specimen of the oriental love-song. That very voluptuousness of the *Song*, which in previous ages had caused the critic some embarrassment even in its allegorical form, now came to symbolize all that was best in the passionate poetry of the ancient Middle East, inspiring Byron's *Hebrew Melodies* with their description of the biblical

> . . . night
> Of cloudless climes and starry skies

in which Solomon had sung of his love.

5

Enthusiastic Devotions

Certainly the most striking contrast between neo-classicism and romanticism is the change from reason to passion, from detached generalization to highly subjective emotionalism. The Augustan with charm and delicacy recounted such human experiences as possessed universal significance for all mankind, and modestly concealed his more personal feelings beneath classical personification and circumlocution. The romantic bared his soul to the world, displaying the variegated passions which struggled within him. For him, it was the personal, the individual experience which had poetic validity.

In this, once again, he stood closer to the biblical tradition than his neo-classical predecessor. True, the Bible saw in every event its eternal and universal meaning, but it was through the personal vision, suffering, and faith of individual men that this universal meaning was expressed. The Bible offered no philosophical *Enquiry Concerning the Origin of Evil*, but it did relate the tragic suffering of the man Job and his search for meaning in an apparently unjust world. In the Psalms of David one finds not formal prayers but the spiritual outpourings of a devout worshipper, whose cries of distress, testimonies of faith, and ecstatic songs of praise were permeated with his own inner experiences, moulded by the mood of the hour.

Unto thee, O Lord, do I lift up my soul. O my God, I trust in thee: let me not be ashamed, let not mine enemies triumph over me. Yea, let none that wait on thee be ashamed: let them be ashamed which transgress without cause. Show me thy ways, O Lord; teach me thy paths. Lead me in thy truth and teach me; for thou art the God of my salvation; on thee do I wait all the day.[1]

[1] Psalm xxv.

I, me, mine—an individualism which permeates the entire book. It was as a direct emotional expression that the Psalm achieved its effect, and on the one occasion when David was rebuked for indecorous exhibitionism—when Michal his wife despised him for dancing wildly before the ark of the Lord— it was she who was punished by God, while David's unrestrained fervour was condoned.[1]

In this tradition, prayers and hymns modelled on such passionate writing were themselves personal and fervent, and a hallmark of the Judaeo-Christian religious poetry in almost every subsequent age has been its individualism and emotion. Yet in the poetry of the early eighteenth century even religious verse succumbed to the contemporary desire for objectivity. In the hymns of Isaac Watts, one of the least restrained poets of his age, his obvious sincerity comes through to us, but almost at second hand.

> Keep Silence, all created Things,
> And wait your Maker's Nod:
> The Muse stands trembling while she sings
> The Honours of her God.

The muse, with all her classical associations, stands between Watts and God, trembling, as it were, vicariously on his behalf and thus producing the usual neo-classical effect that poet and reader are detached spectators. When first-persons occur, they are, with rare exceptions, strangely generalized—almost impersonalized.

> I am not concerned to know
> What to-morrow fate will do;
> 'Tis enough that I can say
> I've possest myself to-day.

There is a didactic tone about the whole which implies the author's wish for all mankind to imitate him, while the Psalms or, indeed, such religious poems as Donne's *Hymn to God the*

[1] II Samuel vi. For a general survey of the reaction to religious sectarianism, see G. Williamson, 'The Restoration Revolt Against Enthusiasm', *SP*, xxx (1933), 571.

Father are unconscious of the reader, so deeply are the authors involved in their own spiritual struggles.

The impersonalization of religious poetry in this period was the inevitable reaction to the zealous sectarianism of the preceding age with its divinely inspired Arminians, Quakers, Socinians, and Baptists, each claiming the exclusive monopoly of 'inner light'. The false messianism of Lodowicke Muggleton, James Nayler, and John Lacy had left a dark residue of suspicion which spread beyond the bounds of inspirationalism to smother even milder expressions of piety. An age of internecine warfare is not easily given to compromise and the passions as a whole came into disfavour together with the excess. Hobbes, beginning logically enough with the statement that madness is an excess of passion, went on to deduce that '. . . if Excesses be madness, there is no doubt, but the Passions themselves, when they tend to Evil, are degrees of the Same'.[1] Since there was no satisfactory way of distinguishing at precisely what point it began to tend to evil, passion itself, he decided, must be avoided, and he demanded that the poet should speak from the principles of nature and his own meditation instead of claiming '. . . to speak by inspiration like a Bagpipe'.[2] It was simply a plea for reason and restraint, but it placed upon poetry the cold touch of philosophy which was to make Keats shudder.

If one wished to avoid the passions, there was no safer ground than the factual field of empirical science, and the new worship of Reason went hand-in-hand with the scientific enquiry of the Royal Society. There could be no fear that emotions would overwhelm the scientist, and so, after years of intensive introspection, men turned to the new objective notions of truth and reality. Since the gulf between science and literature was as yet small and men were eminent in both fields simultaneously, the impact upon literature of the new scientific philosophy was the more profound. Locke's rationalist theories and philosophy, could be brought to bear upon religion, so that soon John Toland deduced from Locke's work the remarkable

[1] Hobbes, *Leviathan*, ed. M. Oakeshott (Oxford, 1946), p. 47.
[2] Hobbes, *Answer to Davenant* in Spingarn, ii, 59.

doctrine that '. . . there is nothing in the Gospel contrary to reason nor above it, and that no Christian doctrine can be properly called a mystery'.[1] If one sees in religion nothing above reason, then all the world of the spirit which religious fervour reveals to the believer as existing behind and beyond the world of reality is darkened and inaccessible. The inspired visions of the biblical prophets could not find their counterpart amid such rationalized devotions.

The dislike of passion had now infiltrated into poetry, and in a famous couplet Roscommon warned his readers against hearkening to that deceptive Inner Voice:

> Beware what Spirit rages in your breast;
> For ten inspir'd ten thousand are possest.[2]

There were still some who found it difficult to apply Reason consistently as the touchstone of literary excellence, but from Roscommon onward the propriety of avoiding a display of passion had become a basic tenet of neo-classical dogma.

Despite the large proportion of Dryden's verse which is devoted to religious topics, it is with difficulty that we think of him today as a religious poet. Scarcely a trace of passion, and certainly none of religious ecstasy, is to be found in his writings, and so rationalized are his religious beliefs that they appear stilted and artificial. There probably was a spiritual struggle beneath the calm exterior, but in its poetic form—and that is what interests us primarily—it leaves many readers with the conviction that he was a religious sceptic.[3] Nothing can better illustrate the gulf between Milton and Dryden than their treatment of religious themes. As we remarked earlier in a different connection, for Milton the story of Samson evoked such intense self-identification that the brutal figure of the Bible emerges as an inspired projection of the blind Milton, torn like Job between anger at the injustice of heaven and a

---

[1] J. Toland, *Christianity Not Mysterious* (London, 1696).
[2] Roscommon, *Essay on Translated Verse* in Spingarn, ii, 306.
[3] Cf. H. J. C. Grierson, *Cross Currents in English Literature of the Seventeenth Century* (London, 1929), p. 322.

longing for reaffirmation of faith.[1] In *Absalom and Achitophel*, published only ten years later, we find an urbane, cynical exploitation of the Bible as a rather amusing device for enlivening contemporary satire, with a deliberately incongruous depiction of divine participation in human affairs:

> Whether inspir'd by some diviner Lust,
> His father got him with a greater Gust. . . .

It is difficult to draw a line of demarcation between writers whose religious belief failed to penetrate the veil of neoclassical restraint and those who simply lacked such belief. But Weber and Tawney have shown us how far the Church, by a peculiar inversion of Puritan self-abnegation, had surrendered its traditional concern with moral guidance in daily life and become the servant instead of the castigator of the new acquisitive society.[2] There were still a few devoted Parson Adamses—altruistic clergymen prepared to live in poverty and to minister conscientiously to the needs of their parishioners, but the ecclesiastical profession at large had become an undignified scramble for the comparatively few lucrative positions. Before the dying incumbent had breathed his last, fawning petitions and urgent pleas poured in upon the political patrons ultimately responsible for distributing the livings. The ambitious clergyman haunted the centres of political activity in London, leaving his flock in the hands of a miserably underpaid curate. As a court chaplain acrimoniously remarked, if any person of genuine weight rose in the profession, it was 'against all rules of gravity and experience'.[3]

---

[1] Tillyard's *Miltonic Setting* (London, 1949), pp. 85–6, summarizes the play as depicting Samson 'in his Protestant-Stoic citadel' and the Stoicism of the play has been accepted by many critics as axiomatic. But this is true only of the opening lines and ignores the change in '. . . restless thoughts that, like a deadly swarm/Of hornets armed, no sooner found alone/But rush upon me thronging', which introduces the Jobian struggle.

[2] R. H. Tawney, *Religion and the Rise of Capitalism* (West Drayton, 1948), especially pp. 252 f. Tawney develops Max Weber's essay, *The Protestant Ethic and the Spirit of Capitalism*.

[3] Quoted in G. R. Cragg, *The Church and the Age of Reason* (Harmondsworth, 1960), p. 120. I owe the Watts quotation to Mr. Cragg as well.

Such subservience to political expediency automatically robbed the Church of its moral leadership. While a fierce theological dispute broke out between the embryonic Deists and the traditionalists, even the latter had been infected by the Latitudinarian translation of religion into a series of ethical rules defensible on purely rationalistic grounds. That rigorous asceticism and harsh self-discipline which had animated the religious sectarianism of the previous century was now transformed into a comfortable, prudential morality tinged at times with a condescending sympathy for the sick and suffering poor, provided that they kept their place, learnt to be industrious, and were duly grateful for the favours received from the rich. Even Isaac Watts could write into a hymn the unsavoury philosophy:

> What though I be low and mean,
> I'll engage the rich to love me,
> While I'm modest, neat and clean,
> And submit when they reprove me.

Thomas Sherlock, the Bishop of London, declared in 1727 in connection with the slave trade that 'Christianity and the embracing of the Gospel does not make the least difference in civil property'—a remarkable statement when one recalls the detailed laws of civil property in the Old Testament, if not in the Gospels. Then again, he explains the acceptance of Christianity in the crudest gambling terms, on the grounds that it is ten to one religion is true, so that if the believer is proved wrong he has lost only one-tenth of the stake, whereas the sinner, if proved wrong has lost far more.[1]

Could one wonder that audiences were not inspired by such preaching? On one occasion a bishop, impressed by the actor's ability to move his audience, asked Garrick why clergymen, though believing what they preached, met with little response, while Garrick, knowing his subject to be only a fable, could rouse his audience. Garrick replied neatly—and only too truthfully—that actors deliver their fictions with the warmth and energy of truth, while ministers '. . . pronounce the most

[1] Quoted in J. E. V. Crofts, *Eighteenth Century Literature: an Oxford Miscellany* (Oxford, 1909).

solemn truths with as much coldness and languor as if they were the most trivial fictions'.[1] The fault was not always on the side of the preachers, for if an occasional note of devotion or fervour crept into a sermon, it was regarded askance by the congregation. James Beattie thought the English temperament unsuited to enthusiasm and drew a vivid picture of the 'inspired' preacher whose sudden apostrophe to the immortal powers or to the walls of his church tended to produce a smile rather than a tear, adding that '. . . there is nothing in the subject and should be nothing in the orator to warrant such . . . vehemence of emotion'.[2] Ignoring the passionate denunciations of the prophets, the devotion of the Psalmist and the long tradition of the sermon as a soul-stirring call for repentance, Beattie required no more of his preacher than a calm, rational proof of the validity of Christianity.

The Church, therefore, had succumbed so completely to the revolt against enthusiasm that it had replaced the passionate individualism of the Bible, and particularly of the Psalms, by a corporate system of ethical formulae. In this setting neither religious poetry nor, for that matter, religion itself could flourish long, and that devotion, which had been trampled down within the Church itself, blossomed in the evangelical movement outside, drawing its nourishment from the fervent songs and prayers of the Psalms. The gracious self-assurance of Augustanism began to be replaced by a sense of helplessness and insufficiency, coupled with a joyful trust in heavenly aid. For the more sanguine poets such as Thomson, Toplady, Smart and the Methodist hymnists, such joy was the impetus for a paean to the Creator of the World, for songs pulsating with gratitude, fervour, and, above all, passion, which had no use for the formal generalities of contemporary hymns.[3]

---

[1] P. Hall, *Sermons and Other Remains of Robert Lowth* (London, 1834), p. 40.

[2] J. Beattie, *Essay on Poetry and Musick* (Edinburgh, 1776), p. 553.

[3] The parallel melancholy mood, expressed in the graveyard poetry of the age, owes its source to the Puritan gloom of an earlier generation inherited by many of the Nonconformists. See E. M. Sickels, *The Gloomy Egoist* (New York, 1932) and A. L. Reed, *The Background to Gray's 'Elegy'* (New York, 1924).

There were signs of the growing need for an emotional outlet in poetry before the Methodists began their work. Dennis,
an early rebel against reason, coupled his plea for passion in
literature with the demand that it should derive its inspiration
from religion. In his *Advancement and Reformation of Modern
Poetry* (1701) he propounded the theory that '. . . passion is
the chief thing in poetry, and that the spirit of genius, and in
short, everything that moves is passion', and he proceeded to
prove that, since a sacred poem is more susceptible of passion,
it must therefore be potentially a greater poem. This 'proof'
suffers from the usual malady of the age, that of reducing personal opinion to dogmatic rule, but his desire for greater
religious passion in verse in order to raise it from the dullness
of Reason was significant. It suggested that from religion
alone could come a revitalization of poetry. However, it was
a theory without illustration and without any clear indica-
tions of the method by which success could be achieved, and
the plea produced no practical results. Within the next few
years a small group of writers subscribed to the theory that
poetry needed greater 'enthusiasm' and 'inspiration' but they
created little more than a ripple on the surface of the general
consensus. Edward Young stated that '. . . thought, enthusiasm and picture' were the '. . . body, soul and robe of poetry',
thus assigning to enthusiasm the role of the soul; Thomson, in
his preface to *Winter* (1728) demanded that poetry '. . . be
inspired from heaven, and, in return, her incense ascend
thither'; and Blackwell declared that the poet ' . . . must screw
up his Fancy so as to smother his Reason'.[1] But the first
important work which was to produce concrete results was
William Law's *A Serious Call to a Devout and Holy Life* (1729).

It was a powerful call for a return to holiness and, from
the effect it had on his young friends John and Charles
Wesley, it may be regarded as the first work in the history of
Methodism. Its primary purpose was religious, not literary,
but in demanding devotion in religion, Law emphasized the
need for singing and the need for joy—in fact the three

[1] E. Young, *Of Lyric Poetry* (1728) and T. Blackwell, *Enquiry into the
Life and Writings of Homer* (London, 1735), p. 278.

essential ingredients of the Psalms on which so many of the Methodist hymns were later to be based; devotion, singing, and joy, all in the service of God. Songs of praise, he declares, '. . . kindle an *holy* flame, they turn your heart into an *altar*, your prayers into an *incense*, and carry them as a sweet smelling savour to the throne of Grace'.[1] In this passage he hints at the superfluity of an altar when the heart is filled with the glory of God, and, in fact, the Methodist movement, partly through force of circumstances but partly also through natural instinct, moved out of the Church into the fields, coming into closer contact with the splendours of creation.

The emotional appeal of Methodism depended largely, as Law had suggested, on community hymn singing, and the brothers Wesley, particularly the younger, provided a wealth of new hymns. In these they caught the spirit of the Psalms not by consciously imitating or paraphrasing them as had their predecessors but, like the Psalmist, by finding their themes within their own emotional experiences. The art of hymnody in the early part of the century had concerned itself with public rather than private emotion not only because of the moderation of tone needed in appealing to universal reason, but also because religious themes were felt to be too lofty for the mortal poet. Samuel Johnson maintained that 'Poetry loses its lustre and its power because it is applied to something more excellent than itself',[2] and remarked of Watts that his devotional poetry was, like that of others, unsatisfactory since the paucity of topics enforces perpetual repetition.

To dismiss religious experience as too limited a subject for verse was a singularly blind judgement, which would automatically condemn a large proportion of some of the best English poetry. The same might well be said about love-poetry, but the diversity of love-poems, like that of religious verse, depends not on the subject-matter itself so much as the approach, the imagery, the mood and diction and, in fact,

[1] W. Law, *A Serious Call to a Devout and Holy Life* (London, 1729), p. 276.
[2] Johnson, *Life of Waller*, where he is echoing a remark of Lord Shaftesbury in the latter's *Characteristicks* (London, 1711), i, 389.

everything that makes for poetry. At all events, Johnson him-self wrote no religious poetry, and his *Prayers and Meditations* was a prose work.

Behind Johnson's refusal to write religious poetry and his conviction that religion was too noble to be put into verse lies the eighteenth century's black and white distinction between mortal and immortal authors; that is, between contemporary authors and biblical. The authors of the Bible were regarded as haloed figures inspired directly from heaven, and therefore not to be imitated by mere humans. An age of rules and of Reason is concerned primarily with definitions and hence with limits. The 'enthusiast' knew no bounds and believed himself capable of anything, but the rationalist recognized his limitations and adapted himself to his circumstances. In the great Chain of Being, man existed on the narrow isthmus between the beasts and the angels and to attempt to write psalms was rather like trying to fly. One could paraphrase, translate, or even imitate, but to write a new set of psalms based on one's own religious experiences was beyond the limits of man.

So long as the biblical poet was regarded as a haloed figure, the critic could hardly urge the contemporary poet to choose religious themes, nor the preacher persuade his flock to follow the example of men who received, at first hand, divine guid-ance in times of trouble. The new interest in the Hebrews as an ancient oriental people living their simple agricultural life helped to present a fresh picture of the biblical characters as ordinary men struggling to live in accordance with the highest moral vision and finding God deep within themselves. The doctrine of election so prominent in the early seventeenth century, whereby Puritans and others identified themselves with biblical characters, and found parallels in their own lives, had disappeared with the rising contempt for 'enthusiasm'; and the idea of building Jerusalem in England's green and pleasant land was, as yet, an aspiration entirely foreign to the eighteenth-century mind. Until men thought of the Bible as a literature inspired by God, but inspired in the hearts of normal human beings, there could be no real bond between David pleading for forgiveness and the repentant sinner of the

eighteenth century; nor, indeed, between David composing his
Psalms and Cowper his *Olney Hymns.*

The divorce between religion and morality owed its existence largely to this very divorce between the Bible and its
readers; for the sins and tribulations of the ancient Hebrews
seemed to have little bearing on behaviour in the age of enlightenment. As the moral link became strengthened by the
growing sense of identity with the ancient Hebrews, so did
the literary bonds. For the first time in the century it was
noted that, although the writings of Moses, David and Isaiah
all bore the mark of the divine impulse, the particular character of each remained clearly visible.[1] Once they were conceived
of as human, the eighteenth-century poet could attempt to
imitate the prophets and the Psalmist, confident that the
sacred theme, so far from swamping his style, would raise it,
and perhaps hopeful of some vicarious inspiration for himself.

Before the Methodists, there was little religious verse
written in the century that did more than provide didactic
discourses on moral and spiritual rectitude, though occasionally, lurking behind the formal exterior, one can glimpse personal emotion struggling for expression. In Addison's poem:

> When all thy Mercies, O my God,
>   My rising Soul surveys,
> Transported with the View, I'm lost,
>   In Wonder, Love and Praise.
>
> O how shall Words with equal Warmth
>   Thy gratitude declare
> That glows within my ravished Heart?
>   But Thou canst read it there.

the poem begins formally enough, but by the second stanza
emotion creeps in and almost overcomes the Augustan
restraint.

Even in the hymns of Isaac Watts, impressive though they
may be, one must look hard for personal expression of individual feeling which has not been generalized almost beyond
recognition, and it is from Charles Wesley's *Jesu, Lover of my
Soul* (1740) that we must date the first hymn of the century

[1] Lowth, *Lecture,* xvi.

in which subjectivity and passion appear undisguised as the motive power of the poem. The stanza:

> Other refuge have I none:
> Hangs my helpless soul on Thee:
> Leave, ah! leave me not alone,
> Still support and comfort me.

is a vivid expression of personal humility and dependence, the *Leave, ah! leave* being the catch in the throat of a worshipper wholly absorbed in his prayer, unconscious of everything but himself and his God. True, these poems were for community hymn-singing, but in the first instance they were written as personal poems and their use in the communal service was intended to help each individual worshipper capture the same personal intimacy with God. Later in the same hymn emerge emotional tones suggestive of romantic poetry.

> Wilt thou not regard my call?
> Wilt thou not accept my prayer?
> Lo! I sink, I faint, I fall!

It presents a picture of spiritual prostration before the object of adoration not far removed from Shelley's:

> O lift me from the grass!
> I die! I faint! I fail!
> Let thy love in kisses rain
> On my lips and eyelids pale.[1]

Indeed the very picture Charles Wesley draws of himself hanging helpless on God is totally at variance with the self-reliance and, at least external, confidence of the neo-classicist. And it is a spiritual prostration stemming directly from such Psalms as:

Save me, O God; for the waters are come unto my soul. I sink in deep mire, where there is no standing: I am come into deep waters, where the floods overflow me.

The subjectivity of the Psalms to which we referred at the beginning of the chapter, expressed in the profusion of first-persons, is reflected clearly in the Methodist hymns as a whole,

[1] Shelley, *Indian Serenade*. Vincent Freimarck notes the similarity in his unpublished thesis.

and a glance at any index to the Wesleyan hymns reveals how far individualism was the hallmark of such hymnody.

I call, I cry, I adore, I believe, I rise, I revere, I groan, I languish, I despair, I lose myself, I lie dead in trespasses; my soul, my heart, my fears, my sleep, my strength, my cry, my sins, my dissolutions; talk to me, stand by me, perform in me, bless me, reveal Thyself to me, be a shield to me.[1]

The helplessness and self-abasement in this Psalmist tradition is linked to romantic poetry by more than mere emotionalism. Central to biblical thought is the realization of man's ambivalent position in the world. On the one hand his sense of inadequacy before the immense powers of Nature prompts him to wonder how God can deign to consider so puny a creature—'What is Man that Thou shouldst know him?' Yet at the same moment the knowledge that God has indeed considered him, has created him in the divine image and made his salvation or damnation a matter of intimate concern lends man a sense of comfort, dignity and joy. And there is a similar emotional ambivalence in Shelley's prostration before the West Wind, in Wordsworth's yearning for moral revitalization from the natural world, and in Coleridge's projection of himself into the mystic seer atoning for his sin against the moral forces of the universe.

Outside the Church, then, the passion and 'enthusiasm' suppressed for so long was expressing itself in religious poetry, and within the Church itself there were now signs that the dominance of reasoned restraint was drawing to a close. Bishop Lowth, soon to be offered the primacy of England, lectured on *The Sublime of Passion* in biblical poetry on the firm assumption that the Bible's superiority over contemporary verse lay largely in its greater fervour and intensity. Indeed, his definition of Hebrew poetry reads like an even more ambitious programme for the romantics than was to appear nearly fifty years later in the preface to the *Lyrical Ballads*.

[1] Cf. E. M. Horning, *Evidences of the Romantic Treatment of Religious Elements in Late Eighteenth Century Minor Poetry* (Washington, 1932), p. 73.

Instead of disguising the secret feelings of the author, he writes, biblical poetry lays them open to public view;

. . . and the veil being, as it were, suddenly removed, all the affections and emotions of the soul, its sudden impulses, its lofty sallies and irregularities are conspicuously displayed.[1]

Within the Church, hymnody soon came to strip off the veil in much the same way as it had among the Methodists, and Augustus Toplady, a bitter opponent of the Wesleys, wrote at times with similar passion and supplication:

> Nothing in my hand I bring,
> Simply to Thy Cross I cling;
> Naked come to Thee for dress;
> Helpless look to Thee for grace.

Again prostration and utter dependence upon God, and the very word *Naked* in so prominent a position shows how far removed the poem is from the 'decently' periphrastic poetry of the Augustans.

The subjectivity of these hymns and their effect upon secular verse can perhaps best be seen in Cowper's *Olney Hymns*. These, although in the evangelical tradition and written in collaboration with an evangelical clergyman, were, in fact, not really intended for corporate singing but were personal, religious poems, reflections of Cowper's own hopes, fears and joys. There is much of the passion of the Psalmist in the lines:

> Help me to reach the distant goal;
> Confirm my feeble knee;
> Pity the sickness of a soul
> That faints for love of thee.

Once more the fainting before the throne of God and the longing to be raised, but here the poignancy is greater, for the poem was prompted not by a passing mood or pious thought but by the desperate turmoil within, the terror of damnation almost swamping the faint hope of forgiveness. It is still a melancholy prayer, dwelling more upon the faintness of the hope than the conviction of ultimate salvation.

[1] *Lecture*, xiv.

In Smart and Blake, however, the more joyful aspect of the Psalms is visible—the paean of praise to be found in such passages as:

Praise him with the sound of the trumpet; praise him with the psaltery and harp. Praise him with the timbrel and dance; praise him with stringed instruments and organs. Praise him upon the loud cymbals: praise him upon the high sounding cymbals. Let every thing that hath breath praise the Lord. Praise ye the Lord,[1]

and the *Jubilate Agno* is, in fact, a series of variations on this very theme. A closer examination of these elements in Cowper, Smart and Blake will be found in the final chapter.

The 'enthusiasm' and passion which, basing itself upon the biblical tradition of personal inspiration from God, had so disrupted the seventeenth century, had thus produced a reaction which excluded such passion not only from poetry in general, but from religious poetry too. Such passion is an integral part of the personal relationship existing between man and God, and it was inevitable that religious verse would be the first to reveal the need for it. And, indeed, so it was; for the dead weight of rationalization within the Church merely drove such verse-writing outside, and the evangelical movement, taking the Bible and, in particular, the book of Psalms as its model, provided the earliest examples of subjectivity and emotionalism in eighteenth-century poetry. It was this which led ultimately to the religious, prophetic poet exemplified by Blake who, spurning the rule of Reason, relied upon his own indwelling inspiration to guide him, declaring

Reynolds's Opinion was that Genius May be Taught & that all Pretence to Inspiration is a Lie & a Deceit, to say the least of it. For if it is a Deceit, the whole Bible is Madness.[2]

And therein lay the most forceful answer to the opponents of 'enthusiasm'.

[1] Psalm cl.
[2] Blake, *Notes on Reynolds*, in *Poetry and Prose*, ed. G. Keynes (London, 1943), p. 779.

6

The Boundless Universe

(1)

The emotional subjectivity of romantic verse expressed itself largely in the poet's response to the evocative powers of nature and in the mystic bond which he felt existed between the lonely, craggy steeps and his own sense of spiritual isolation. Nature had come alive, and from the vernal wood came strange moral impulses, felt in the blood and along the heart, which suggested that amidst the sky, trees and flowers there lurked a Spirit of the Universe—awesome and magnificent, yet at the same time a source of comfort and joy. Romanticism is essentially pantheistic; but it is never far removed from the Hebraic concept of the world as the creation of a just, benevolent God. The distinction between pantheism and divine immanence is at best a fine one. If there was theological significance in the antinomian trends of a Deism which shaded off into pantheism, for the poet it mattered comparatively little whether the moral impulses came from a Nature which embodied or which testified to the deity. The Psalms are permeated with the vision of the heavens relating the glory of the Lord, and the Hebrew poet, like the romantic, found in the visible world of nature and, more precisely, in his sense of comparative insignificance beside it, an awareness of his own moral duties and of the spiritual and social equality of all men before the Creator. In the changing tastes of the eighteenth century, in the movement away from the classical pastoral tradition and towards romantic pantheism, it was to the Bible that the poet frequently turned for this response to divine immanence; and the new sensitivity to the sublime magnificence of nature echoes in almost every instance the sentiments and, indeed, the very phrases of the Psalms to which it was so profoundly indebted.

Broadly speaking, the nature idealized in the earlier part of the century was either the idyllic scene of the pastoral, or the countryside in balmy weather viewed as a pleasing background to human activity. Nature was artistically subordinated to man, and Richard Wilson's painting of 'The Thames near Twickenham', with its two or three small figures in the foreground adding the human interest to a quiet stretch of the river, contrasts vividly with Turner's 'Calais Pier' which at the end of the century depicted a tempestuous scene of mountainous waves tossing the mariners' frail craft against the wooden pier. The earlier tradition of nature tamed was never more clearly visible than in the landscape-gardening of William Kent and Capability Brown, who surrounded the stately eighteenth-century home with a landscape apparently natural but in fact carefully planned to combine the maximum aesthetic satisfaction with the minimum offence to delicacy and refinement. From the artificial dam neatly hidden behind the trees, the stream wound gently along its artificial channel to cascade over an artificial waterfall—yet all in the name of nature.

The reflection in poetry of the dichotomy between real and stylized nature needs little demonstration here. Every reader knows that while Johnson might yearn to lie

> . . . where o'er the verdant ground
> Her living carpet nature spreads.

in real life he could be persuaded only with the greatest difficulty to leave his beloved London. It was a pleasant game to translate the moonrise into terms of Celia mounting the vaulted sky, but the reality of the countryside fell far short of the charming picture created in verse. Lady Montagu, in one of those moments of candour rare in her age, put into the mouth of Melantha the peevish complaint:

> How simple was I to believe
> Delusive poetical dreams,

Or the flattering landscapes they give
Of meadows and murmuring streams.
Bleak mountains and cold starving rocks
Are the wretched results of my pains,
The swains greater brutes than their flocks;
The nymphs as polite as the swains.[1]

The *murmuring streams, nymphs* and *swains* were all part of
the mechanics of contemporary verse which deliberately
widened the gap between art and nature, while it was still
obstinately maintained that Nature and Art were the same—
and this, as Professor Lovejoy has shown, it was easy to do
with so elastic a word as *nature*.[2] Ambrose Philips, who was as
guilty of the faults he criticized as any of his contemporaries,
amusingly parodied this aesthetic artificialization of nature:

To blooming Phyllis I a song compose
And, for a rhyme, compare her to the Rose.
Then, while my fancy works, I write down Morn
To paint the blush that does her cheeks adorn.
And when the whiteness of her skin I show
With extasy bethink myself of Snow.

Nature was there to provide the palette from which poetry
could receive its bright touches of colour; but in fact
the complaint was justified that 'We live within Doors,
cover'd, as it were, from *Nature's Face*; and passing our days
supinely ignorant of her Beauties.'[3]

In the conventional neo-classical poem, the birds warbled
their lays in shady woods while Corydon sang of his love. In
contrast to this stands the Nature of the Bible, in which the
lion roars for his prey, the vulture sucks the blood of the slain,
and both tremble before the power of God. The world is seen
and portrayed in all its glory and in all its terror; not only in
the peace of a quiet morning, but also in the raging storm at
sea, when the winds, God's messengers, cast mountainous

[1] Lady Mary Wortley Montagu, *Letters and Works*, ed. W. Moy
Thomas (London, 1893), ii, 489.

[2] See A. O. Lovejoy, 'Nature as an Aesthetic Norm', in his *Essays in
the History of Ideas* (Baltimore, 1948).

[3] A. Philips, *Epistle to a Friend*, and T. Blackwell, *Enquiry into the
Life and Writings of Homer* (London, 1735), p. 25.

billows over the frail decks and the mariners pray desperately for salvation. Through the strength and vigour of the natural scene is perceived the power of the master hand. Any idyllic picture of wolves lying down with lambs is reserved for the messianic era, but in the world as we know it, even so gentle a poem of faith as *The Lord is my shepherd* draws its contrast from the valley of the shadow of death. And the distinction between the neo-classical view of nature and the biblical is, by and large, the difference between the coy nymphs of *Windsor Forest* and the fearful symmetry of Blake's magnificent Tyger.

The statement that the neo-classicist was interested only in nature artificialized does, of course, require some modification. James Sutherland and others have reminded us that much of Augustan poetry dealt with the beauties and even the terrors of nature and that such poets as Thomson, Dyer, Shenstone, and even Pope himself wrote with admiration of the simple charms of the countryside.[1] But there is an important distinction to be made—a distinction made only too rarely—between what I have termed the 'palette' technique and genuine nature poetry. For the eighteenth-century poet usually saw nature through the spectacles of books, and if we are to talk of movement towards romanticism, the first criterion must be the attempt to capture in poetry a direct emotional response to the natural world.

Shenstone does indeed turn away from the town to the delights of the country, but like that landscape-gardening to which he himself was so devoted, his verse is methodized into art.

> Whether we fringe the sloping hill
> Or smooth below the verdant mead;
> Whether we break the falling rill
> Or through meand'ring mazes lead.

As the title of the poem, *Rural Elegance*, suggests, the countryside becomes charming when man, the artist, has finished

[1] James Sutherland, *A Preface to Eighteenth-Century Poetry*, pp. 158 f. D. Nichol Smith has an interesting article on the Scottish source of Thomson's sensitivity to nature in his *Some Observations on Eighteenth-Century Poetry* (Toronto, 1937), p. 56.

fringing and smoothing it. Similarly, Pope's famed version of Horace's ode

> Happy the man whose wish and care
> A few paternal acres bound

skilfully recaptures the 'rural retreat' theme of the original— it expresses a passing mood of dissatisfaction with the town; but for all that, it betrays no serious longing for the countryside. The lines

> Whose herds with milk, whose fields with bread,
>   Whose flocks supply him with attire;
> Whose trees in summer yield him shade,
>   In winter fire.

are, to any sensitive reader, lines written in the study by a poet thinking in abstract terms about the distant countryside. They are not the vivid response of a nature lover. And we should remind ourselves again that this is not a failing in Pope, but a difference in sensibility, a tendency to subdue emotion to art rather than to find art in emotion.

Thomson himself, quoted so frequently as evidence of the fresh naturalism to be found within Augustanism, is only rarely a genuine nature poet. There are in his writings, as we shall examine in a moment, some very real instances of emotional involvement with nature, but the kind of passage usually cited simply does not stand up to closer scrutiny. A frequent illustration of early 'sublime horror' in nature runs:

> Now the black tempest strikes the astonish'd eyes;
> Now down the steep the flashing torrent flies;
> The trembling sun now plays o'er ocean blue,
> And now rude mountains frown amid the skies.

We notice that it is not the poet but the impersonal observer's *astonish'd eyes* which are struck; the lightness of the word *flies* is one which no direct viewer would apply to a cascading torrent; by a witty allusion to its reflection in the water, the sun itself is depicted as *trembling*; and the repeated word *now* confirms our suspicion that the poet is, as it were, touching up a painting with a brush-stroke here, a dab there. If we are too obtuse to perceive the palette technique, he informs us in the following lines:

> Whate'er Lorrain light touch'd with softening hue,
> Or savage Rosa dash'd, or learned Poussin drew.

Indeed, it was Thomson himself who described it as his aim to '. . . meditate the Book of Nature'.

To give one final instance, we hear repeatedly of the 'awful solemnity' apparent in Parnell's *Night Pieces*,[1] but again we must ask how valid the term is. His best-remembered passage reads:

> How deep yon azure dyes the sky!
> Where orbs of gold unnumber'd lie,
> While thro' their ranks in silver pride
> The nether crescent seems to glide.
> The slumb'ring breeze forgets to breathe,
> The lake is smooth and clear beneath,
> Where once again the spangled show
> Descends to meet our eyes below.
> The grounds which on the right aspire,
> In dimness from the view retire;
> The left presents a place of graves,
> Whose wall the silent water laves.
> That steeple guides thy doubtful sight
> Among the livid gleams of night.

The dominant impression is less that of awful solemnity than of a tour around a pre-arranged 'walk'. The stars are a *spangled show* cleverly reflected in the lake to provide that element of mild surprise beloved by the landscape gardeners. The left-hand side of the scene *presents* a graveyard to the viewer, and the steeple *guides thy doubtful sight* towards other interesting points.

All this is not to suggest that Thomson, Parnell and others were blind to the power and splendour of the natural scene. But we should be wary of accepting too glibly the theory that the 'local' poetry of Dyer, the *Night Pieces* of Parnell, and the nature poetry of Thomson showed that neo-classical verse

[1] See for example, Norman Callan, 'Augustan Reflective Poetry' in the Pelican Guide, *From Dryden to Johnson*, ed. Boris Ford (Harmondsworth, 1957), p. 353.

allowed room for vivid poetic responses to the natural world. In the major portion of their work such poets adopted the current techniques of transmuting these responses into formal art, and only rarely did their enthusiasm break through convention to lend a note of rapture to their verse. It is in this sense that we are entitled to speak of such rarer instances as adumbrations of romanticism.

It was, then, in the less 'tamable' aspects of the natural scene—the bleak mountains, the tempests and the lonely moors—that the gulf lay between neo-classicism and Hebraeo-romanticism, and behind the former view was a vexed theological problem. In his *Telluris Theoria Sacra* (1681–9), Thomas Burnet had argued the Calvinist view that the 'imperfections' in nature resulted from original sin. John Keill replied that these imperfections, by which were meant the 'ugly' protuberances of rocks and mountains, had their utility in the economy of nature, in accordance with the Psalmist's dictum that '. . . the high hills are a refuge for the wild goats and the rocks for the conies'. Though they differed in their theological explanations, both sides began from the assumption that mountains and precipices were 'warts and excrescences'; as Burnet put it, ' . . . a Ruin that is fresh, looks much worse than afterwards, when the Earth grows discolour'd and skinn'd over. But I fancy, if we had seen the Mountains when they were new born and raw, when the Earth was fresh broken, and the Waters of the Deluge newly retir'd, the Fractions and Confusion of them would have appear'd very ghastly and frightful.'[1]

This antipathy to mountains stems, as Marjorie Nicolson has pointed out in a recent book, from New Testament sources.

Whether in external Nature or in the social scene, what was 'high' was suspect; what was 'low' more worthy. Mountains were 'high', 'rough', 'crooked', symbolic of a perverse generation. Into

---

[1] T. Burnet, *Sacred Theory of the Earth* (London, 1726), i, 195–6, and J. Keill, *An Examination of Dr. Burnet's Theory of the Earth* (Oxford, 1698). On the duality of Burnet's responses, see B. Willey, *Eighteenth-Century Background* (Harmondsworth, 1962), p. 34.

them was read a social philosophy implied in verses in Luke: 'He hath put down princes from their thrones; and hath exalted them of low degree. . . .' Many English Puritans, living in a time of political and social change and chaos, read into mountains and valleys their own equalitarian philosophy.[1]

But conversely the Old Testament, unconcerned with the later Christian doctrine of original sin and unaffected by the later identification of valleys with Christian humility, tended to ennoble the mountains. The awesome might of the hills was the scene of Abraham's sacrifice, of the Ten Commandments, of the blessing and cursing of the people on their entry into the Promised Land. Indeed, so deep was the veneration for such hills that they became only too frequently the sites of idolatrous altars. Yet even such idolatry failed to detract from their splendour, and the poetry of the Bible is filled with tributes to the sense of comfort and faith which they inspired when man lifted his eyes unto the hills from whence his help came.

The eighteenth-century love of order, unity, and form limited the world of literature, as far as was practicable, to those areas of the globe normally inhabited by men. In contrast, the pre-romantic exploitation of the awful, the horrific, and the untamable cultivated a sense of the vastness of creation and of man's dwarfishness beside it. His interest was directed to those uninhabited mountain peaks, those barren deserts and stormy oceans which had fascinated the Psalmist; and in almost every early example of this new view, the Psalms were quoted directly or allusively as the source or at least the precedent for the feeling of awe and terror before the grandeur of Nature.

Addison was one of the first to respond to the 'sublime horror' of nature untamed:

I cannot see the Heavings of the prodigious Bulk of Waters, even in a Calm, without a very pleasing Astonishment, but when it is worked up in a Tempest, so that the Horizon on every side is

[1] Marjorie H. Nicolson, *Mountain Gloom and Mountain Glory* (Ithaca, 1959), p. 42. See also J. C. Shairp, *On the Poetic Interpretation of Nature* (Edinburgh, 1877), and C. A. Moore, 'The Return to Nature in English Poetry of the Eighteenth Century', *SP*, xiv (1917).

nothing but foaming Billows and floating Mountains, it is impossible to describe the agreeable Horrour that arises from such a Prospect.[1]

This comment has been widely quoted by critics as a *locus classicus* for the new admiration of stormy scenes. But it has not been noted that his sentiment serves merely to introduce the storm description in Psalm cvii which he prefers 'before any other I have ever met with'. He then quotes at length:

They that go down to the sea in ships, that do business in great waters; these see the works of the Lord and his wonders in the deep. For he commandeth and raiseth the stormy wind, which lifteth up the waters thereof. They mount up to the heaven, they go down again to the depths; their soul is melted because of trouble. They reel to and fro, and stagger like drunken men and are at their wit's end.

Addison's own version of the Psalm rounds off the essay.

The biblical passage which runs like a scarlet thread through these early examples of 'agreeable Horrour' is Psalm civ and, particularly, the verse which vividly portrays God

> . . . who maketh the
> clouds his chariot; who walketh upon the
> wings of the wind.

Thomson, although he sprinkled his *Seasons* liberally with conventional periphrases and mythological personifications, displayed nevertheless a genuine love of nature in its immensity and power as well as in its quieter moods. The Calvinist talk of 'imperfections' he dismissed contemptuously with the words:

> Let no presuming impious railer tax
> Creative Wisdom, as if aught were formed
> In vain, or not for admirable ends.[2]

and himself wrote with almost Davidic rapture of that grandeur of untamed nature which reveals the master hand.

> Oh! talk of him in solitary glooms,
> Where, o'er the rock, the scarcely-waving pine

---

[1] *Spectator*, No. 489.
[2] J. Thomson, *Summer*, 318.

Fills the brown shade with a religious awe.
And ye, whose bolder tone is heard afar,
Who shake the astonished world, lift high to Heaven
The impetuous song, and say from whom you rage . . .
. . . and thou, majestic main,
A secret world of wonders in thyself,
Sound his stupendous praise, whose greater voice
Or bids you roar, or bids your roaring fall.[1]

The feeling inspired by such scenes is a 'religious awe' and nature has become animated, lifting its voice and praising its Maker, just as in the Psalms themselves, in an ecstasy of devotion. And as though to assure us that this is no pantheistic paean, but a song to the biblical God, he alludes to Psalm civ, addressing God as

> . . . on the whirlwind's wing
> riding sublime.[2]

Gray went even further, insisting that the grandeur of nature at its most impressive was itself a proof of divine creation more effective than any philosophical speculation.

Not a precipice, not a torrent, not a cliff but is pregnant with religion and poetry. There are certain scenes that would awe an atheist into belief without help of other arguments.[3]

For Gray, as for the Psalmist, such moving natural scenes were pregnant not only with religion but also with poetry. But his feeling is predominantly one of solemnity, and his Jeremiah-like Bard sets the tone for his lamentation with a reminder of the fearful might of wild nature:

> Hark, how each giant-oak, and desert cave,
> Sighs to the torrent's awful voice beneath!

A strain of mournful piety runs through most of these early eulogies of the grandeur of nature, but from the Methodist movement came signs of a more joyful attitude. James Hervey, in his *Reflections in a Flower Garden* (1746), wrote of the garden turning preacher, of the flowers delivering lively ser-

---

[1] *Hymn to the Seasons*, 42. [2] Ibid., 18.
[3] Gray, *Letter to Richard West*, 16 November 1739, in *Correspondence*, ed. P. Toynbee and L. Whibley (Oxford, 1935), i, 128.

mons and, in the phrases of the Psalmist, he exclaimed: 'While the little hills clap their hands and the luxuriant valleys laugh and sing, who can forbear catching the general joy?' This animation of nature is a harbinger of Wordsworth's daffodils tossing their heads in sprightly dance and outdoing the sparkling waves in glee.

Cowper, only half within the evangelical movement, never succeeded completely in surrendering to the joy of fervent devotion. It was with greater seriousness that the ocean affected him, leaving him '. . . with lasting impressions of the awful Power that created and controls it.'[1] But though he might not burst out into hallelujahs, he felt a quiet confidence and trust, almost a family pride when he gazed on the work of God, saying of the true believer:

> His are the mountains, and the valleys his,
> And the resplendent rivers; his to enjoy
> With a propriety that none can feel,
> But who, with filial confidence inspired
> Can lift to heaven an unpresumptuous eye
> And smiling say—My Father made them all.[2]

In his most famous hymn, *God moves in a mysterious way*, we again hear echoes of Psalm civ in the description of God who

> . . . plants his footsteps in the sea
> And rides upon the storm.

And this same biblical image, which impressed itself so deeply upon these pre-romantics, appears yet again when Burns informed a friend that '. . . a stormy wind howling among the trees and raving over the plain' provides him with the best season for devotion since his mind is then '. . . rapt up in a kind of enthusiasm to *Him* who . . . walks on the wings of the wind.'[3]

Such horrific scenes were the new source of religious inspiration and the Irish poet, Thomas Moore, wrote from Niagara

---

[1] Cowper, *Letter to William Unwin*, 26 September 1781, in *Selected Letters*, ed. M. van Doren (New York, 1951), p. 71.

[2] Cowper, *Task*, v, 747 f.

[3] Burns, *Letter to Robert Riddel*, April 1784, in *Complete Works*, ed. A. Cunningham (Boston, 1856), p. 318.

Falls of the unforgettable feeling of terror which gripped him when he first saw their grandeur and magnificence, adding 'My whole heart and soul ascended towards the Divinity in a swell of devout admiration, which I never before experienced. Oh! bring the atheist here, and he cannot return an atheist.'

Storms, howling winds, heaving oceans and towering mountains as well as the simpler joys of nature in her calmer moods were now sources for poetic inspiration in place of the artificial, idyllic scenes of pastoral verse. Seen in its newer, unsophisticated form, Nature recalled to the viewer both the solemnity and the rapture of the Scriptures, thereby providing authoritative support for the poet in an age when such attitudes to nature were strange and eccentric.

Repeatedly within the verse of the romantic poets themselves one hears more than an echo of such religious experience as Thomson, Gray, and Cowper had drawn from the roaring winds and heaving ocean. Byron addresses the ocean as

> Thou glorious mirror, where the Almighty's form
> Glasses itself in tempests . . .
> . . . boundless, endless and sublime,
> The image of eternity, the throne
> Of the Invisible.[1]

It is the immensity of God which he sees reflected in the tempestuous seas and this very idea of the reflection, the image in the waters, reveals that his is not the pantheistic view of nature which often appears in the poetry of Wordsworth. Coleridge borders between pantheism and Hebraism when he urges the reader to

> . . . see and hear
> The lovely shapes and sounds intelligible
> Of that eternal language, which thy God
> Utters, who from eternity doth teach
> Himself in all, and all things in himself.[2]

But even Wordsworth, despite the pantheism implicit in such phrases as

> God and Nature's single sovereignty

---

[1] Byron, *Childe Harold*, iv, 183.   [2] Coleridge, *The Nightingale*, 98.

returned in later life to the biblical sources of his pantheism, changing the above line in his 1850 version of the *Prelude* to:

> Presences of God's mysterious power,
> Made manifest in Nature's sovereignty.

Only a few lines needed to be altered here and there to transform the pantheistic approach to nature into a Christian attitude.[1]

Throughout these passages one hears the cadences of the Psalmist marvelling at the God who makes clouds his chariots and walks on the wings of the wind; at whose rebuke the sea flees and at the voice of whose thunder the waters hasten away. If we pause for a moment to compare this view of nature with that prevailing at the beginning of the century:

> See Pan with flocks, with fruits Pomona crown'd
> Here blushing Flora paints the enamell'd ground,
> Here Ceres' gifts in waving prospect stand.
> And nodding tempt the joyful reaper's hand,[2]

we shall see how far we have come. Flocks, fruits, flowers and corn all offering their contributions to Man, the highest on earth in the scale of Being, and the whole scene translated into charming mythological terms. To turn from this to Blake's *Tyger* is to turn from the classics to the Bible; to the Hebraic sense of man's insignificance in the awesome grandeur of creation, which perceived behind the physical world the powers of Good and Evil struggling for supremacy before the throne of the supreme judge and creator of the universe. And all this echoing the biblical sense of wonder:

> Did He, who made the Lamb, make thee?

(II)

In any discussion of 'nature' in pre-romanticism, the words *awe*, *grandeur* and *immensity* are bound to recur, and this change in sensibility is closely linked to what the eighteenth century called the *sublime*, with its connotations of terror,

---

[1] Wordsworth, *Prelude*, ix, 237, in Selincourt, ed. p. 320. See also H. N. Fairchild, *Religious Trends*, iii, 252–3.

[2] Pope, *Windsor Forest*, 37. For the analogy with Eden in this passage, see T. R. Edwards, Jr., *This Dark Estate* (Berkeley, 1963), p. 7.

might and magnificence. The treatise *On the Sublime* attributed to Longinus, which began its influence on European literature with Boileau's translation, appealed to Boileau and his followers primarily because of its systematic analysis of literary effects and the implication that careful attention to these various aspects of sublimity would result in literary work of the highest merit. It was the old classical search for ultimate standards of literary excellence, appealing to a generation seeking guidance and adopting the same static view of literature.

But there were in this treatise many concepts troublesome to the neo-classicist, such as Longinus's insistence that the sublime 'throws an audience into transport' and 'with strength irresistible, strikes home and triumphs over every hearer.' For the neo-classicist it was not difficult to turn a blind eye to these minor difficulties and concentrate on Longinus's demand for rules and regulations. But under the aegis of this magical word *sublime*, implying as it did the authority of the classical Longinus, subtle variations of the neo-classical interpretation led finally to the indulgence in terror and mystery which marked among other things the Gothic novel, still under the name of the *sublime*.

A passage which caused particular trouble was that which helped to link sublimity with the Bible in the eighteenth century: the passage in which Longinus praised the effectiveness of the simple verse *And God said, Let there be light; and there was light.* In fact, Longinus's only comment was the vague remark that the Jewish lawgiver, when he had conceived a just idea of the Deity, expressed it appropriately; but this rare example of a classical authority commenting upon the Holy Scriptures, and commenting favourably, was seized upon with avid interest. Huet and Le Clerc were puzzled by the contradiction between the simplicity of the biblical verse and the grandeur which they felt Longinus demanded in sublime passages, maintaining that Longinus had erred in defining the verse as sublime. But Boileau came staunchly to the defence of the Bible, and on the latter's authority the English neo-classicists accepted unquestioningly the view that the style of the Bible not only conformed to Longinus's definition of sublimity, but was an excellent model for it. John Dennis, who propounded one of the earliest theories of the Longinian sublime in England, developed Boileau's view by declaring that all forms of the sublime were ultimately religious in source. The sun, he informs us, may appear in fact no more than a flat circle approximately two feet in diameter, but in meditation it suggests '. . . a vast and glorious Body, the top of all visible Creation, and the brightest material image of the Divinity.'[1]

The most important single contribution to the eighteenth-century ideas of the sublime was the famous annotated translation of Longinus by William Smith, Dean of Chester, which appeared in 1739 and went through five editions in the century. It was from this translation onward that the sublime became linked with grandeur, awe, and terror, and it was largely in Smith's version that subsequent readers came to know Longinus. But as they read the translation, their attention was drawn on almost every page to his footnotes explaining and illustrating the theory, amongst which notes the Old Testament figured as the noblest illustration he could offer for the sublime. In one passage, for instance, Longinus praises Homer's description of the earth trembling at the advent of a Greek god:

> Fierce as he past, the lofty mountains nod,
> The forests shake, earth trembled as he trod
> And felt the footsteps of th' immortal God.

Smith at once comments that the Scriptures do the same far more effectively, suggesting for comparison Psalm xviii, 7:

Then the earth shook and trembled, the foundations also of the hills moved, and were shaken, because he was wroth. There went up a smoke out of his nostrils and fire out of his mouth devoured: coals were kindled at it. He bowed the Heavens also and came

---

[1] J. Dennis, 'The Grounds of Criticism in Poetry', in *Works*, ed. E. N. Hooker (Baltimore, 1939–43), i, 339. See also S. H. Monk's monumental work *The Sublime* (New York, 1935), p. 49. W. J. Hipple's *The Beautiful, the Sublime, and the Picturesque* (Carbondale, 1957) makes no mention of the biblical source of the eighteenth-century sublime.

down, and darkness was under his feet. And he rode upon a cherub, and did fly, and came flying upon the wings of the wind.

It is true that Pope's translation of Homer which Smith quotes scarcely does justice to the original, but this served merely to heighten the contrast to the detriment of the classics.

In all there were about twenty such biblical references in the notes to this edition, but the most remarkable is that in which he compares the ghosts and apparitions of Elizabethan tragedy, with a 'fine specimen' in the book of Job:

In thoughts from the visions of the night, when deep sleep falleth on men, fear came upon me, and trembling which made all my bones to shake: Then a spirit passed before my face, the hair of my flesh stood up. It stood still, but I could not discern the form thereof: an image—before mine eyes—silence—and I heard a voice,—Shall mortal man be more just than God?

At a time when the horrific sublime was as yet foreign to eighteenth-century taste, Smith admired this 'Gothic' passage from the Bible and, we may note, he deliberately emphasized the mystery and terror by subtle changes in punctuation. He omitted the connectives of the Authorized Version, such as '. . . and I heard a voice, *saying*', substituting dashes to increase the dramatic effect. When Burke produced his influential *Philosophical Enquiry into the Sublime and the Beautiful* (1756) with its advocacy of mystery and terror, he seized upon this same passage, describing its incomprehensible darkness as amazingly sublime, '. . . more awful, more striking, more terrible than the liveliest description, than the clearest painting could possibly represent it.' The connection between such terror and mystery and the scenes with which Gothic novels abound is patent—the dark corridor at night, the almost indistinguishable shape flitting silently along, the horrific thrill and the sudden silence, all trading upon the new delight in such gruesome description.

The idea of applying Longinus's principles to the Bible was exploited at great length by Lowth who, although he added little to the theory of the sublime, yet underlined the connection with the Bible by introducing the word *sublime* into the titles of six of his lectures as well as into the lectures themselves. Two months after the publication of the lectures, Joseph Warton took up the idea in a novel fashion by writing two letters to the *Adventurer* purporting to announce that he had discovered a new manuscript by Longinus written after he had become acquainted with the whole of the Old Testament. In these letters the supposed Longinus is 'greatly astonished' at the sublimity of the Bible which excels the finest examples of classical literature, and the point is illustrated by a profusion of quotations. Significantly, Longinus is made to declare that had he known the whole of the Bible before he wrote his treatise on the sublime, he would have changed many of its principles. In other words, instead of the Bible being judged by Longinus's principles, Longinus was now being judged by the literary standards of the Bible.

The change in aesthetic standards during the eighteenth century was effected largely by those twin Proteuses of neoclassical criticism—*nature* and the *sublime*, which shifted their meaning completely during this period. By the end of the century, as they both appear in romantic poetry, they are linked by the sense of awesome grandeur in the natural scene, the feeling that the physical world in its 'uncivilized' form was replete with moral lessons, solemn and somewhat terrifying. By the time of the romantic poets themselves the biblical sources were scarcely visible, but the Davidic idea of the mountains and valleys coming to life in order to praise their creator and fulfil his commands had contributed to the new view of an animate nature. The biblical description of the immensity of God's power in creation had helped to lead poets' thoughts to the beauty of lonely crags and barren moors. And Coleridge, writing of this new view of the sublime, was prompted to declare:

Could you ever discover anything sublime in our sense of the term in the classical Greek literature? Sublimity is Hebrew by birth.[1]

[1] Coleridge, *Table Talk and Omniana*, ed. T. Ashe (London, 1884), p. 174.

7

The Bible Poetized

The preceding chapters have attempted to examine those elements in Hebrew poetry which contrasted with neoclassical theory and hence offered the pre-romantic new models for his own creative writing. But before the biblical tangibility of metaphor or the Psalmist's animation of nature could capture the imagination of the new school of writers, such metaphors and emotions had to be seen in their simple, unveiled state and not clothed in the heavy disguise of heroic couplets. So long as it was believed that the poetry of the Bible depended upon an accentual metre which had been lost in the course of time, the biblical translator felt bound to replace the metre by one of his own—usually the heroic couplet. This superimposed metre served merely to intensify the current practice of converting the individual style of foreign poems into that of the neo-classical, and obscured almost completely the native simplicity, vividness and passion of biblical writing.

Until this veil had been removed, the pre-romantic could not turn to Hebrew poetry for inspiration, but only to the diffuse Augustan translations—for at this time the Authorized Version was regarded as merely a prose translation, useless as a poetic model. The discovery of parallelism revealed that, in fact, the best method of retaining the peculiar quality of biblical verse—the pulsating rhythm of ideas and feelings— was in a literal prose translation and that, therefore, the Authorized Version was a valid model for poetic forms.

The wordy biblical paraphrases of the eighteenth century reflected the more general picture of Augustan translation. To

126

the neo-classicist, translation meant more than transference from one language to another. It meant the right to alter style, diction, atmosphere and general effect until the original conformed to the accepted literary standards of the day. In Procrustean fashion, the critics had decided upon the correct aesthetic measurements and chopped or stretched the originals until they fitted snugly into place. For the most part, instead of looking directly to the classics for corroboration of their literary maxims, they looked to contemporary translations, finding there, not surprisingly, a style remarkably akin to their own.[1]

Horace's advice in the *Ars Poetica* not to follow one's original too slavishly was quoted repeatedly as authority for the flights of fancy inserted into paraphrases. Sir John Denham took this advice even further when he insisted that, since poetry is so very subtle and cannot be transferred from language to language, it was the duty of the translator to infuse 'a new spirit' to replace that of the original. Similarly, Dryden felt some pride in claiming that, in his translation of Chaucer, '. . . what beauties I lose in some places, I give to others which had them not originally', and Johnson regarded it as axiomatic that Pope needed to '. . . colour the images and point the sentiments of his author' when translating the *Iliad*.[2] In general the translator excused any liberties he might take with his original either because a literal version was dull or because he felt duty-bound to rouse a nodding Homer. The result was that all translations, from whatever original source, sounded much the same, and the complaint could be heard later in the century that translators have only one style and that Homer, Vergil, Horace and Ovid '. . . are compelled to speak in the same numbers and in the same unvaried expression.'[3] What was worse, even authors of entirely

[1] Although the British Museum catalogue is not exhaustive, the fact that it records for the eighteenth century only six Greek editions of the *Iliad* as against thirty-one complete or partial renderings, suggests a wider interest in translations than in originals.

[2] See the essay accompanying Denham's translation of *Aeneid*, ii, Dryden's *Preface to the Fables*, and Johnson's *Life of Pope*.

[3] P. Francis, *A Poetical Translation of Horace* (London, 1750).

different cultures and civilizations were made to sound the same, and without the author's heading *Ode in Imitation of . . .* it is frequently difficult, if not impossible, to determine the original model of a paraphrase. Johnson's lines:

> Year chases year, decay pursues decay,
> Still drops some joy from with'ring life away;
> New forms arise, and diff'rent views engage,
> Superfluous lags the veteran on the stage,

differ little from:

> Amidst the drowsy charms of dull delight
> Year chases year with unremitted flight,
> Till want now following, fraudulent and slow,
> Shall spring to seize thee like an ambush'd foe,

and yet the first he wrote in imitation of Juvenal and the second as a paraphrase of Proverbs. The eighteenth-century poet had reason to gaze complacently at the host of contemporary translations and to imagine that he had found the key to all great literature; for there before him were the most venerated writers of the world adopting the very standards of elegance and decorum of which his age had laid down the rules.

There is an amusing illustration of this process of transmogrification in James Beattie's suggestion that the line from *Othello*:

> My mother had a maid called Barbara

would, if translated by a neo-classicist, become:

> Even now, sad Memory to my thoughts recalls
> The nymph Dione, who with pious care,
> My much-loved mother, in my vernal years
> Attended.[1]

As long as it was impossible to distinguish any essential difference between Juvenal and Proverbs in neo-classical paraphrases, there was little that the Bible could offer the pre-romantic poet. The popularity of verbose paraphrases of the Bible is even more striking when one recalls that there was always a literal prose version available for those wishing to know the original. The Authorized Version had injected the

[1] J. Beattie, *Essay on Poetry and Musick* (Edinburgh, 1776), p. 543 n.

beauty of its phrases and rhythms into the very substance of the English language and it was at the same time treasured as a triumph of Jacobean prose. The paraphrasing of biblical passages, therefore, arose from the conviction that something had been lost in the translation into English. For, although the images, subject-matter and style of the Authorized Version were, at times, highly poetic, the eighteenth-century hesitated to call it poetry. It would not scan and, what was perhaps worse, it contradicted the neo-classical rules.

Milton obligingly supplies us with some neatly documented evidence of the techniques of seventeenth-century paraphrase. In 1648, he wrote versions of nine Psalms in metrical form, italicizing all words which did not appear in the original Hebrew. His purpose was, of course, to draw attention to those words which were translated directly from Holy Writ and hence had special significance, but it is more to our purpose to note how many words were introduced which do not appear in the original.

> Thou Shepherd that dost Israel *keep*
> Give ear *in time of need*
> Who leadest like a flock of sheep
> Thy loved Joseph's seed.

> That sitt'st between the Cherubs *bright*
> *Between their wings outspread*
> Shine forth *and from thy cloud give light*
> *And on our foes thy dread.*

More than two-thirds of the second stanza is pure invention, and yet this was a serious attempt by a leading Hebraist of the day to achieve fidelity to the original text.

The version of the Psalms published in 1696 by Nahum Tate and Nicholas Brady, which proved enormously popular for many years, contains many worse attempts. In their edition the verse:

> The Lord is my shepherd I shall not want

becomes:

> The Lord himself, the mighty Lord
> Vouchsafes to be my guide.

The shepherd by whose constant care
My wants are all supplied.

The stark simplicity of the biblical verse creates an immediate picture of simple unwavering faith—and it is a simplicity essential in an image depicting the poet as the trusting, guileless sheep. In the paraphrase all this is lost, and so sophisticated a word as *vouchsafes*, with its implication of God's condescension, destroys the beauty and charm of the original. The paraphrase has the advantage, of course, that it can be sung to a hymn tune, but the numerous versions in heroic couplets do not have even this excuse.

Sir Richard Blackmore's version of *Job*, despite its lengthy preface denouncing the classical source of contemporary verse, was nevertheless modelled on the classical epic and far removed from the original Hebrew. Thus the verse.

Why died I not from the womb? Why perished I not when I came forth from the belly?

is toned down to meet the requirements of decorum by abstract nouns and personification:

> Why did a false conception not elude
> My parent's hopes and Life from me exclude?
> Why was I shap'd and fashioned as a Man?
> Why Life not stifled when it first began?

In 1712, Addison published his rendering of Psalm xxiii, in which the verse 'He maketh me to lie down in green pastures; he leadeth me beside the still waters' emerges as:

> When in the sultry Glebe I faint,
> Or on the thirsty Mountain pant;
> To fertile Vales and dewy Meads
> My weary wand'ring Steps he leads;
> Where peaceful Rivers, soft and slow,
> Amid the verdant Landskip flow.[1]

In the introduction to this paraphrase he makes the illuminating comment that this Psalm is '. . . a kind of *Pastoral* Hymn, and filled with those Allusions which are usual in that kind of writing.' He has obliged us by confirming in black and white

---

[1] *Spectator*, No. 441.

our suspicion that the neo-classicist judged foreign literatures largely by their contemporary paraphrases. Addison's version is indeed filled with those allusions typical of the eighteenth-century pastoral—the *sultry Glebe*, the *fertile Vales*, the *dewy Meads*, and the *verdant Landskip*. But where, we are entitled to ask, do they appear in the original? We are reminded of Dr. Bentley's comment on Pope's *Iliad*—'It is a pretty poem, Mr. Pope; but you must not call it Homer.' Pope's own *Messiah*, published in the same year as Addison's paraphrase, follows the Miltonic tradition of biblical subject-matter in classical form.

Perhaps one last clinical specimen will illustrate the diffuse paraphrases best, since it combines almost all the defects of such translations while yet remaining perfectly respectable neo-classical verse. The Authorized Version has for a verse in Psalm cxxxix:

If I ascend up into heaven, thou art there; if I make my bed in hell, behold thou art there.

This a minor poet of the age paraphrased as:

> If thro' the Sky I urge my rapid Flight
> To regions blazing with immortal Light,
> 'Tis there the Seraph owns thy scepter's Sway
> Thy Glory beams intolerable Day.
> Or if to Hell I bend my downward course,
> Thy Justice there exerts its dreadful Force.
> Thy terrors howl around the dismal Cave,
> And frighted Devils tremble and believe.[1]

The length of the passage has been trebled and the additions are elaborations derived from the poet's imagination and not from the Psalmist's. In the first couplet alone, *ascend* is replaced by the conventional Latinate circumlocution *urge my rapid flight*, and similarly *heaven* is expanded into *regions blazing with immortal light*. As a result, the directness, the swiftness and the passion of the original become weighed down by cumbersome periphrases and expansions until nothing is left of the Hebraic spirit.

It would be superfluous to give further illustration of the

[1] T. Drummond, *Poems Sacred to Religion and Virtue* (London, 1756).

biblical paraphrases with which the early part of the century abounded. They appeared as modest offerings to patrons, as contributions to periodicals, or as the life-work of obscure clergymen. Good or bad, they retained very little of the spirit of Hebrew poetry and could offer nothing fresh to a poet seeking a new model for his verse.

Among the earliest critics of these paraphrases was Aaron Hill who, in 1720, remarked that the simplicity of Hebrew poetry was usually lost '. . . by our mistaken Endeavours, after heightening the Sentiments, by a figurative Expression.' This, he felt, might help the leanness of some contemporary compositions, but '. . . to shadow over the Lustre of a divine Hebrew Thought by an Affectation of enliv'ning it, is to paint upon a Diamond, and call it an Ornament.'[1] His own effort, however, fell dismally short of his excellent observations and revealed that, greatly though he respected and admired biblical style, he still felt the diamond needed a coat of paint before it became verse.

A decade later, John Husbands' *Preface to a Miscellany of Poems* (1731) noted how much better Hebrew verse survived literal translation than did other languages and praised its vivid use of metaphor. Yet quoted amid high commendation was a very poor translation of Psalm xviii by Sternhold in which

Then the earth shook and trembled; the foundations also of the hills moved and were shaken because he was wroth

was rendered

> Such in his power that in his wrath
> He made the earth to quake,
> Yea, the foundations of the Mount
> Of Basan for to shake.

Quite apart from the clumsy ending, it has substituted a theological statement for the Psalmist's vivid attribution of a natural phenomenon to its cause. At all events, Husbands revealed again the gulf between the theoretical recognition of the Bible's poetic merits and its practical application in biblical translation.

[1] Aaron Hill's preface to *Creation*, ed. cit., p. 4.

In fact, until parallelism had been identified, there could be no significant change, and the biblical paraphrases would have needed to wait until a more general literary move towards simplicity could affect them. By its rediscovery, however, the biblical versions took on the vivid quality of the Hebrew original long before such changes were visible in secular verse, and hence were able to exert a positive influence upon the trends towards romanticism. It was a stroke of good fortune that the discoverer of parallelism was not merely a Hebraic scholar but a leading literary critic of his day, a renowned classicist and a man sufficiently admired and respected to be able to champion the Hebraic verse-forms without calling down upon himself the kind of ridicule which had greeted Addison's championing of *Chevy Chace*. And, what is more, in demanding absolute fidelity in biblical translation, he himself provided an example for his readers which was at once adopted as a model for later versions.

Lowth's theory of translation was, to a certain extent, implicit in his exposition of parallelism; for if the poetic character of Hebrew poetry depended not upon metre but upon the balance of ideas and phrases, the translator was better advised to retain this specific poetic character in a literal version than to compensate for the supposed loss of metre by translating into heroic couplets. Like Aaron Hill, Lowth noted how much better Hebrew stood up to translation than did the classics, but unlike his predecessors, he was able to explain the phenomenon. For on the basis of parallelism it was now clear that, provided the same general form of the sentence was retained, the rhythmic pattern of thought would be visible in the translation. His comment was no longer the academic point made by Hill, but a serious warning that, with Hebrew far more than any other original, the aim must be to translate, 'as far as may be, in equivalent words, phrases and sentences.'[1]

In the lectures themselves it was difficult for Lowth to provide models of the kind of translation he demanded, since the lectures were delivered in Latin and, in any case, as a classi-

---

[1] *Preliminary Dissertation to Isaiah* (London, 1778), p. lii.

cist, he was expected to provide tasteful translations into Latin hexameters. In this he was tempted and fell, offering translations which, by being in a quantitative metre lost their value as faithful versions. However, on the occasions when he abandoned metre his translation was surprisingly close to the original. For the famous passage from the *Song of Songs,*

Rise up, my love, my fair one, and come away. For lo, the winter is past, the rain is over and gone, the flowers appear on the earth; the time of the singing [of birds] is come, and the voice of the turtle is heard in our land,

he has

Surge age, Deliciae meae!
Formosa mea, et veni!
Ecce enim, Hyems praeteriit;
Pluvia enim, tempestas transit, abiit:
Apparent humi flosculi:
Tempus adest cantus avium;
Et vox Turturis in terra nostra auditur.

Unlike the Vulgate translation, this retains the syncopated rhythm of the original, and the brief sentences are placed together as in the Hebrew to create an almost breathless excitement which is yet smooth and wonderfully musical.

This last example contains a change in the principle of biblical translation whose importance can scarcely be over-emphasized. Although it has the appearance of metrical verse and is set out as such, it is, in fact, poetic prose devoid of any regular metre. Behind this change lay the whole theory of parallelism and on it was based Lowth's own translation of Isaiah and the numerous imitations which were to follow it. Lowth had now shown that the poetic quality of Hebrew verse lay not in its metres but in its parallelism of sense-units and that, therefore, a literal prose translation preserved the original poetic form more closely than any rendition into metre. He was, however, faced with a problem. If he left it in prose form, the fact that it was, in fact, 'biblical' verse would escape notice. He decided therefore to compromise by translating into prose and setting the prose out line by line to indicate that it nevertheless constituted verse It was a decision which, as we shall see, affected profoundly the writings of Macpherson, Smart and Blake.

This device was used to the full in the translation of Isaiah which he published in 1778—a version which was at once acclaimed as a landmark in biblical translation. A comparison of the opening verses of the Authorized Version and of this translation will indicate most clearly the change involved:

The Authorized Version begins:

1. The vision of Isaiah the son of Amoz, which he saw concerning Judah and Jerusalem in the days of Uzziah, Jotham, Ahaz *and* Hezekiah, Kings of Judah.

2. Hear, O heavens, and give ear, O earth; for the Lord hath spoken. I have nourished and brought up children, and they have rebelled against me.

3. The ox knoweth his owner, and the ass his master's crib; *but* Israel doth not know, my people doth not consider.

In the Hebrew and, indeed, in the English, it is clear from the absence of parallelist rhythm that the first verse is merely a prose superscription introducing the prophecy, while the vision itself, beginning with the second verse, is poetry. In the above quotation no difference is indicated, but Lowth's version begins:

CHAPTER

1   THE VISION OF ISAIAH THE SON OF AMOTZ,
WHICH HE SAW CONCERNING JUDAH AND JERUSALEM;
IN THE DAYS OF UZZIAH, JOTHAM, AHAZ, HEZEKIAH,
KINGS OF JUDAH.

2   Hear, O ye heavens; and give ear, O earth!
For it is JEHOVAH that speaketh.
I have nourished children and brought them up;
And even they have revolted from me.

3   The ox knoweth his possessor;
And the ass the crib of his lord:
But Israel knoweth not Me;
Neither doth my people consider.

In this version not only are the lines set out to emphasize the parallelism, but whenever it can be done without torturing English usage unduly, Lowth chooses phrases which will echo the original word-order and hence retain the parallelism. Thus he avoids the more normal *master's crib* of the Authorized Version, preferring *the crib of his lord* in order to retain the parallel of *ass* in *Israel*, and of *lord* in *Me*. This is not pedantry but a perception of the essential quality of Hebrew poetry. In this passage it is precisely the image of Israel as the foolish ass failing to recognize its master that forms the central theme of the chapter, reflected in the structure of the verse itself.

We have only to compare this version with any contemporary translation of the same passage in order to see not only the greater fidelity to the original, but also the success achieved in retaining as far as was humanly possible the poetic quality of the original. William Langhorne begins:

> Jehovah speaks—let all creation hear!
> Thou Earth attend! ye rolling Heavens give Ear!
> Reared by my Care and fostered by my Hand
> My rebel sons against their Father stand.

Isaiah's magnificent call to heaven and earth as eternal witnesses, with its allusion to Deuteronomy xxxv, is here relegated to second place and, what is worse, the personal declaration of God, the passionate denunciation in the first-person, is blunted by *their Father* which produces the usual effect of detachment and non-involvement. Of biblical parallelism there is no trace, except insofar as it happens to coincide with the neat balance of the heroic couplet, and the directness and simplicity of the original has, as usual, been replaced by the sophistication of neo-classical verse.

The gap between Lowth's presentation of the theory of parallelism in 1753 and his own translation of Isaiah in 1778 was marked by numerous attempts to follow the translation theory implicit in parallelism, but such attempts revealed a reluctance to carry the theory completely into practice as Lowth was to do later. Even such attempts as were made formed only a small proportion of the rather dull, verbose paraphrases produced by conscientious and industrious clergymen and poetasters, not yet awake to the new theory of translation. Percy's translation of the *Song of Songs*, to which we have had cause to refer more than once, marked a turning-point in biblical translation. Giving due credit to Lowth, Percy proceeded to translate the Song into prose, set out as a dialogue between the husband and the spouse with the virgins forming a chorus. The latter device indicates by its dependence upon Greek drama that the tradition of drawing classical parallels to the Bible was slow to die, but the virtue of the translation was its fidelity to the original and its recognition that the best method of retaining the original spirit was by translating into prose.

The new emphasis on the passion and fervour of Hebraic poetry was linked with the 'wild' Pindaric, and the year after Percy's *Song* a Pindaric version of Moses' song on crossing the Red Sea appeared which, although redistributing the parallelism, remained far closer to the original than most previous translations, and succeeded in retaining much of the excitement of the biblical passage. One stanza runs:

> Thy right hand, O Lord
> So glorious in Power! be ever adored;
> Thy right hand in pieces hath dashed the proud Foe;
> The rebels who rose
> Thy will to oppose
> Thou didst in thine excellent greatness o'erthrow;
> The breath of thine Ire
> Consum'd them like Stubble devour'd by the Fire,[1]

and it will be noted that the biblical image of God's anger consuming them like stubble is left untouched. It was thus that the images and diction of the Bible, quite apart from its verse forms, could be perceived and admired as poetic models.

Once Lowth's *Isaiah* had appeared, translators had a practical example to follow and results were soon forthcoming. Alexander Geddes brought out a *Prospectus of a New Translation of the Hebrew Bible* (1786) praising Lowth's work lavishly and, in effect, suggesting that the same principles of translation as had guided him should be applied to a translation of the rest of the Holy Scriptures. Individual translations appeared, such as Benjamin Blayney's *Jeremiah* of 1784 which was a conscious attempt to provide a sequel to Lowth's

---

[1] L. Abbot, *Poems on Various Subjects* (Nottingham, 1765).

work. The accuracy of such translations, the distinction (for the most part correct) between the prose and poetic sections of the Hebrew and the setting out of the latter line by line but without metre, showed that the lessons had been well learned.

The change that had occurred in verse translations is illustrated by an excellent version of Psalm xv which appeared in the *Gentleman's Magazine* of 1786 over the name Edwin Goodwin. It succeeded in rendering the Psalm suitable for hymnal purposes while yet retaining the charm and simplicity of the original almost unimpaired. There is no infusion of 'a new spirit' such as Denham had suggested, but a successful attempt to preserve the original spirit as far as possible.

> Lord! who shall in thy temple rest
>   Or on thy hill abide?
> A man sincere, whose deeds are just
>   And words by truth are tried.
>
> Whose tongue hath ne'er detraction known
>   Who seeks no neighbour's ill
> Who ne'er indulges causeless wrath
>   Whose ear no slanders fill.
>
> Who usury will ne'er receive
>   Nor bribes to wrong the pure:
> He who his duty thus pursues
>   Shall stand for evermore.

In metrical translation it is inevitable that some changes in word-order and even in choice of words become necessary, particularly when the verse is rhymed; and a careful comparison of this poem with the Hebrew reveals that such licence has been taken. But what is most noticeable is that there has been no deliberate attempt to introduce extraneous material and to 'render' the passage into something different. This point had been noticed by James Beattie who, after remarking on the difficulty of translating biblical passages into verse for hymnal purposes, attacked the needless paraphrases of Tate and Brady who had inserted meaningless epithets into almost every line:

> The chariot of the King of Kings
> Which *active* troops of angels drew,
> On a strong tempest's *rapid* wings,
> With *most amazing* swiftness flew.

The italics are his and indicate words which had been introduced for no reason other than to impart a more 'poetic' flavour to the original. But a comment which he adds as a humorous afterthought—'Nay, I am in doubt whether Church musick would not have more energy, if we were to sing our psalms in prose'[1]—has more truth in it than he himself realized. For it was only when psalms were in fact translated into prose set out as verse that the true poetic quality of the original could be appreciated.

As a summary of the changes which took place in biblical translations during the century, it is valuable to compare various versions of the same Psalm in chronological order and to watch the move from diffuseness and periphrasis towards literal and accurate renderings. Let us take as our example the well-known opening of Psalm cxxi:

> I will lift up mine eyes unto the hills, from whence cometh my help; my help cometh from the Lord which made heaven and earth.

Nahum Tate's version of 1696 is very far from this:

> To Sion's Hills I lift my eyes
> From thence expecting Aid
> From Sion's Hill and Sion's God
> Who Heaven and Earth has made.

Here the vivid image of insignificant man gazing up at the hills as a symbol of might is exchanged for the theological dogma that it is the God of Zion only who is the creator of the world, *Sion* becoming the key word in place of the original *help*. The hills are no longer any hills, but are specified as the Holy Mount, again emphasizing theology rather than faith. In addition the introduction of *expecting*, which appears nowhere

---

[1] J. Beattie, *Letter to Blair on Psalmody* (written 1778 and published 1839), p. 6. See also his *Essay on Poetry and Musick*, ed. cit., p. 419.

in the original, creates a note of uncertainty totally at variance with the deep faith which pervades the Hebrew.

Isaac Watts' version is even more distant from the original, his fault lying mainly in the superfluous adjectives—the besetting sin of Augustan poetasters.

> To Heaven I lift my waiting Eyes
> There all my hopes are laid.
> The Lord who built the Earth and Skies
> Is my perpetual Aid.

Waiting and *perpetual* are cumbersome, and the pastoral setting implied by the image of the hills is exchanged for *Heaven* as a symbol of God's abode. The *hopes* laid in heaven are very different from the simple statement of the Hebrew, and the dependence on God for help, which is the central theme of the verse is left to the last line of the stanza, almost as an addendum.

In 1765, James Merrick, claiming to be a disciple of Lowth, published one of the most popular psalters of the century, but his translations were still very Augustan in form. The verse we have taken as our example he turned from an intensely sincere soliloquy into a pompous dramatic performance:

> Lo! From the hills my Help descends
> To them I lift my Eyes.
> My strength on him alone depends
> Who formed the Earth and Skies.

Just before the close of the century, a work came into England from Sweden which provided a perfect example of the new type of translation. The author, J. A. Tingstadius, had translated the Psalms into Swedish with great accuracy and fidelity, his version then being rendered anonymously into English. What is most remarkable is that, although the English version was the translation of a translation, so closely did it keep to its Swedish original, also setting out its prose line by line as verse, that the English version is itself a triumph, retaining all that could be desired of the original Hebrew spirit. Moreover, a separate work by Tingstadius leaves no doubt that he was closely in touch with the parallelist theory and fully aware of the new trends in biblical translation. His version of Psalm cxxi is a vast improvement on previous translations, beginning:

> I lift mine eyes up to the mountain
> Whence my help cometh.
> My help cometh from the Lord
> The creator of Heaven and Earth.

Even the slight change of *mountains* to the singular is a slip on the part of the English translator, not Tingstadius.

In our own day, the translation and paraphrasing of biblical passages do not form an important part of a poet's work, but in the eighteenth century there were few poets who did not at some time turn to the Bible for inspiration. For the poets of the earlier part of the century, the Bible provided a storehouse of poetic ideas and allegories which furnished '. . . very noble matter for an Ode', but in the process of clothing such material in the garb of neo-classical verse, the passion and simplicity were almost completely lost. But the theory of parallelism (which showed the poetic quality of what had been previously regarded as prose) led inevitably to a spate of more literal translations, and the literary quality of the Bible, no longer disguised as neo-classical verse, became more clearly visible. As a result, the passion, simplicity and directness of Hebrew poetry, coupled with the views of nature and the sublime which it contained, became more firmly impressed upon the imagination and style first of the pre-romantics and then of the romantic poets themselves.

In addition, the new literal prose-translations set out line by line as verse showed that poetry was not exclusively dependent on accentual metre or rhyme, but could rely to a large extent on poetic imagery and sense-rhythms. The Bible itself, as was now clear, achieved its effect by allowing the passion of the writer to dominate his verse and to carry him along, as it were, in waves of thought, not bound fast to a rigid system. The quantitative metre of Latin hexameters had made necessary for the versifier the use of a *Gradus* to translate his thoughts into periphrases. This practice, when transferred to the English accentual metre, had canalized emotion

141

into artificial channels, and the same technique applied to translation stereotyped all literature as Augustan in form. But the new insistence upon literal versions of the Bible which showed that true poetry could be so free from metre as to be almost indistinguishable from prose in outward form, gave the pre-romantics a new pattern for their own creative writing—the songs, hymns and prophecies of the Hebrew Bible.

8

The Trumpet of a Prophecy

(1)

It is time now to stand back a little from the canvas and try to see the picture as a whole. When all is said and done, when we have spoken of the Bible's role in the primitivist movement, in the development of imagery and of all those more detailed aspects of poetry which together form the background to the creative writing of the age, what are the changes in secular poetry itself that can be attributed to the new acceptance of the Bible as a literary model? What verse-writing owes its poetic techniques, its subject-matter and its emotional resonance in part or in whole to the style and content of Hebraic writing?

Among the most influential of pre-romantic works were those strange poems attributed to Ossian which produced so powerful an impression both in England and on the Continent, fascinating such poets as Goethe with their melancholy longing for the past, their simple dignity and their solemn rhythmic prose. Whether they were translations of an ancient Celtic manuscript or were, as Johnson called them, '. . . as gross an imposition as ever the world was troubled with', it is clear that the style, the imagery and even much of the content was largely the work of James Macpherson and thus was a literary phenomenon of the mid-eighteenth century, reflecting the changing tastes of the age.

It will be noted that this 'translation' of the Ossianic poems was a translation into a rhythmic prose, rhythmic in the sense that it depended upon a rhythm of ideas and feelings rather than of accent:

If on the heath she moved her breast was whiter than the down of Cana; if on the sea-beat shore, than the foam of the rolling ocean. Her eyes were two stars of light, her face was heaven's bow in showers. Her dark hair flowed round it like the streaming clouds.

It was, of course, set out as prose since it purported to be no more than a prose translation. But if one takes such a prose passage and sets it out line by line as verse, the basis of this rhythmic prose is revealed as biblical parallelism itself—a debt reinforced by imagery reminiscent of the *Song of Songs.*

> If on the heath she moved
> > her breast was whiter than the down of Cana;
> if on the sea-beat shore,
> > than the foam of the rolling ocean.
> Her eyes were two stars of light,
> > her face was heaven's bow in showers.
> Her dark hair flowed round it
> > like the streaming clouds.

The Bible was not the only model for Macpherson's translation: there were many, among them Homer and Milton. However, it was the biblical flavour of the translation that convinced many contemporaries of the authenticity of the work, and of the existence of an original manuscript despite Macpherson's inability to produce it. Illogically, they seized upon traces of his biblical model as proof positive of the antiquity of the Ossianic poems, and instead of suspecting that Macpherson had been guilty of plagiarism from the Bible, they pointed triumphantly to the similarities in imagery, in diction, and in passion as evidence of its age. Indeed, if we trace this scriptural affinity to its source, it becomes apparent that those who encouraged Macpherson while he was in the process of composing his 'translation' by admiring the biblical flavour of his work, prompted him to stress it in the subsequent sections.

Dr. Hugh Blair, for example, without whose energetic assistance and encouragement the work would have made almost no impact, had, only a year or two before his advocacy of Macpherson's work, composed his *Lectures on Rhetoric and Belles Lettres* in which he devoted one lecture to the poetry of the Bible.[1] This lecture contained nothing original, being merely an acknowledged reworking of Lowth's lectures with especial emphasis on the contrast between the 'fervid, bold and animated' writing of the Bible and the 'regular correct expression to which our ears are accustomed in Modern Poetry'. But it gave a brief exposition of parallelism and recommended to students a detailed examination of the Scriptures as affording an excellent example of the taste of a remote age and country—a taste very different from that of contemporary literature.

It was not surprising, therefore, that a critic so deeply imbued with the literary qualities of the Bible should welcome as genuine a work purporting to be a translation from an ancient original, but drawing heavily on the style and imagery of the Bible. For the similarities appeared to reveal qualities shared with another primitive masterpiece whose validity could not be questioned. It was Blair who first encouraged Macpherson to prepare for publication the *Fragments of Ancient Poetry collected in the Highlands of Scotland* (1760) and who headed a committee to obtain money for the project. When Johnson and others questioned the authenticity of the later poems, it was Blair again who defended him in his *Critical Dissertation on the Poems of Ossian* (1763) in which he urged as his strongest argument in favour of their authenticity, the vehemence, fire and enthusiasm in which they bore a 'remarkable resemblance' to the style of the Old Testament.

While Blair regarded the biblical similarity as authenticating the work, Malcolm Laing, the most bitter of Macpherson's opponents, later pounced on *The Six Bards* as evidence of plagiarism from Lowth. In this attack, Laing printed the poem twice—once set out as verse in the form transmitted by the author to Gray and Shenstone, and once as prose in the form in which Macpherson had published it.[2] The former presentation drew attention to the parallelist

---

[1] Although the lectures were not published until 1783, a note in the preface sets their date of composition no later than 1759—Blair states he had been delivering them at Edinburgh University for 24 years.

[2] M. Laing, *The Poems of Ossian* (Edinburgh, 1805). The continental influence is examined in P. Van Tieghem, *Ossian en France* (Paris, 1917).

rhythms of what pretended to be prose, and Laing pointed to the theory recently enunciated by Lowth as the obvious source of the poem's success. The fact that in 1753, a few years prior to his first publication and the year in which Lowth's lectures were first published, Macpherson was a divinity student at King's College, Aberdeen, makes it more than likely that he had known of parallelism, and substantiates Laing's suspicions. By the time of Laing's attack, however, the Ossianic poems had already done their work; they had fired the imagination of the pre-romantics in England as well as in France and Germany, and given them a taste for the solemn, exotic rhythms and images of 'primitive' literature, for a verse free from restraint and convention, far removed from the sophistications of classical poetry and closer to the vividness and passion of the Bible.

Yet the Ossianic poems, however profound their effect, might technically be excluded from the category of pre-romantic poetry, first since they purported to be translations, and secondly since they were set out as prose in their published form. Of the pre-romantic poets themselves, three stand out prominently as responding most readily to the changing tastes of the time, particularly those tastes modelled on the Bible—Smart, Cowper, and Blake. There existed between these three poets a peculiar bond; they were all religious visionaries so profoundly involved in their devotional joys and fears that they bordered on insanity. Smart fell on his knees in prayer when and where the mood took him; Cowper writhed at the thought that he was doomed to everlasting perdition; and Blake, coming closest to biblical tradition, chatted amicably with angels and Hebrew patriarchs. In all three this religious obsession expressed itself in the form of intensely personal verse-writing and, as the obsession took a firmer hold, so the individualism became more marked.

In tracing the way in which the Bible fostered the movements of enthusiasm and passion we noted how, even at the highest level, religion had become a matter for solemn reasoning rather than a theme for a Davidic psalm of joy. Rationalism had stifled almost all forms of emotional expression, and

146

melancholy was the prevailing illness. It was in reaction to this aspect of Reason's supremacy that these poets found an emotional outlet in their verse, incidentally blazing a trail for others to follow—Smart in his ecstatic songs of praise, Cowper more gently in his evangelical hymns, and Blake in his prophetic denunciation of social abuse. And as they move farther away from the Reason of neo-classicism, so the style, the imagery and the rhythms of the Bible are more clearly recognizable in their writings.

Smart's interest in the Bible began early in his life. When he took up residence at Cambridge in 1739, he already possessed some knowledge of Hebrew, showed a quick ability in translating from it, and, as the records at Pembroke College show, read the Bible in the original Hebrew. His attention was first drawn to religious themes in poetry by the Seatonian prize which required (with a naïve disregard for divine infinity) a poem on '. . . one or other of the perfections or attributes of the Supreme Being, and so the succeeding years, till the subject be exhausted.' These early poems with which Smart won the prize are Miltonic in character, revealing little originality in structure or content, though filled with frequent allusions to biblical passages. Where these allusions occur, Smart follows the tradition both of his predecessors and of many contemporaries in paraphrasing almost beyond recognition. 'Before I formed thee in the belly I knew thee' becomes:

> When in my mother's womb concealed I lay
> A senseless embryo, then my soul thou knewest.

But there are hints of his later style when he adopts the Psalmist's call to nature to join him in his thanksgiving.

> List ye! how Nature with ten thousand tongues
> Begins the grand thanksgiving, Hail, all hail,
> Ye tenants of the forest and the field!
> My fellow subjects of th' eternal King.
> I gladly join your Mattins, and with you
> Confess his presence, and report his praise.[1]

[1] Smart, *Poems*, ed. R. Brittain (Princeton, 1950), pp. 94 and 91.

In this, however, he has done little more than Thomson in the *Hymn* appended to his *Seasons*. A few years later, he began a verse-translation of the psalter, which was as diffuse and remote from the original as most contemporary translations.

In 1759, however, from the somewhat dull pages of his poetry there suddenly sprang a new phenomenon in eighteenth-century literature—a poem pulsating with adoration and fervour, at times almost incomprehensible in the passionate outpouring of words—the *Jubilate Agno*. It was a wild, ecstatic call to all animals, fish, insects, and birds to join him in praise of the Almighty; a call which scorned all rules and embellishments, adopting instead the fire and rapture of the Psalmist.

What caused this sudden break with the past, this eruption of fervour and passion? Of course, it was his fit of madness, but why should his madness have taken this particular form? The reason is to be found some three years before he wrote the poem, when in 1756 Smart first read Lowth's lectures and was so profoundly impressed by them that in both the January and February issues of his *Universal Visiter* he recommended them enthusiastically to his readers, declaring that '. . . for its elegance, novelty, variety, spirit and (I had almost said) divinity, it is one of the best performances that has been published for a century.'[1] We have seen that Lowth's insistence on parallelism as the basic factor in Hebrew poetry led him to insist on literal prose translations set out as poetry. Macpherson did almost this when translating the Ossianic poems, but his work was (at least ostensibly) a translation. In the *Jubilate Agno*, Smart exploited biblical parallelism for original verse-writing. Here was a poem set out as verse as if it were metrical, but containing no trace of rhyme or metre other than the sense-rhythm by which it achieves its effect.

Rejoice in God, O ye tongues; give glory to the Lord and the Lamb.
Nations and Languages, and every Creature in which is the breath
    of Life.

[1] The first critic to notice this indebtedness was W. F. Stead in his *Rejoice in the Lamb* (London, 1939), p. 297.

> Let man and beast appear before him, and magnify his name
> together.
> Let Noah and his company approach the throne of Grace, and do
> homage to the Ark of their Salvation.

Not merely is this parallelism, but the poem has captured the
excited pulsation of Hebrew poetry. The latter half of each
line seems to lean back on its haunches before leaping forward
with the next thought; and the subject-matter, too, takes us
back to the world of the Old Testament, revitalizing it as
though Abraham and Isaac were standing beside Smart ready
to participate in this universal thanksgiving.

> Let Abraham present a Ram, and worship the God of his Redemp
> tion.
> Let Isaac, the Bridegroom, kneel with his Camels, and bless the
> hope of his pilgrimage.
> Let Jacob, and his speckled Drove adore the good Shepherd of
> Israel.
> Let Esau offer a scape Goat for his seed, and rejoice in the blessing
> of God his father.

The spiritual world is seen as transcending the petty divisions
of chronology and Smart feels himself already a part of the
heavenly host. Indeed, as W. F. Stead has remarked, where
the gentle, innocent Cowper lived in terror of damnation,
Smart, whose personal life was by no means blameless, was
filled with the blissful certainty that he was of the chosen:

> For I am not without authority in my jeopardy, which I derive
> inevitably from the glory of the name of the Lord.
> For I bless God whose name is Jealous—and there is a zeal to
> deliver us from everlasting burnings.
> For in my existimation is good even amongst the slanderers and
> my memory shall arise for a sweet savour unto the Lord.

Like the biblical prophet who despised the mockery and jeer-
ing of his enemies, trusting in the word of God, so Smart
dismissed the objections of those who scorned his 'enthusiasm'
by looking beyond this merely temporal world.

> For my hope is beyond Eternity in the bosom of God my Saviour.
> For by the grace of God I am the Reviver of ADORATION amongst
> ENGLISH-MEN.

For beeing deserted is to have desert in the sight of God and
intitles one to the Lord's merit.
For things that are not in the sight of men are thro' God of infinite
concern.

Even the pun on *desert* shows how completely he had clothed
himself in the biblical mantle. For in an earlier chapter we
noted how overt plays on words in neo-classical poetry were
always intended to win applause for the poet's wit. In Hebrew
poetry, however, they have a metaphysical gravity, suggesting that the affinity of the words is not fortuitous but symptomatic of a deeper affinity of ideas—as in the beating of
swords into *ploughshares*. So here, to be deserted by mankind
is to be exiled into the desert where Elijah and other prophets
spent so much of their time, winning eventually the desert of
God's grace.

Smart's own function was to prophesy to the Englishman
that the period of detached, rationalized devotion was over,
and that an era of joyful worship in the streets as well as the
churches was on its way.

For I prophecy that they will obey the motions of the spirit
descended upon them as at this day.
For they have seen the glory of God already come down upon the
trees.
For I prophecy it will descend upon their heads also.
For I prophecy that the praise of God will be in every man's
mouth in the Publick streets.
For I prophecy that there will be Publick worship in the cross ways
and fields. . . .
For I prophecy that they will learn to take pleasure in glorifying
God with great cheerfulness.

Such, for Smart, was the new concept of poetry—not to relate
'What oft was thought but ne'er so well expressed' but to
write of the glories of heaven where

. . . innumerable Angels fly out at every touch and his tune is a
work of creation.

It was his task, no less, to castigate man for his backsliding
and to insist in the name of God on righteousness and social
justice. If today we may not always sympathize with Smart's

ideals (such as the joyful prophecy that women will '. . . be cooped up and kept under due control') for the most part his plea is for honesty, integrity and compassion:

For I prophecy that there will be more mercy for criminals . . .
For I prophecy that the clergy in particular will set a better example.
For I prophecy that they will not dare to imprison a brother or sister for debt.
For I prophecy that hospitality and temperance will revive.

There is a sadly personal note in his vision of a messianic era in which no one will be imprisoned for debt, and that too forms part of the attempt to find poetry in oneself, in those aspects of life which are of vital personal concern. The way in which the names of personal friends keep popping up among the biblical figures reflects Smart's ability to see his own life and the world around him in terms of the Bible.

Smart's more famous poem, the *Song to David*, has been described as the most romantic poem of its time, and it is in many ways indicative of what might be termed the 'aftermath'. The *Jubilate Agno* is the trumpet-call to battle, the spurning of Reason and the fervent dedication of a new artform which takes the Bible as its model. But when the battle was over and the break had been made, the poet adopted a metrical pattern less revolutionary, yet different in quality from the sophisticated verse on which he had turned his back. The subject is still biblical, the tone reverent, but the poem is calmer and more controlled.

> For ADORATION, DAVID's Psalms
> Lift up the heart to deeds of alms;
>   And he, who kneels and chants,
> Prevails his passions to controul,
> Finds meat and med'cine to the soul
>   Which for translation pants.

The parallelism is not exactly that of the Bible, but it does retain the throb of meaning, the doubling-back on ideas.

> Prevails his passions to controul,
> Finds meat and med'cine to the soul.

which was to play a part in the so-called 'incremental

151

repetition' of romantic poetry. For if the ballads taught the
technique of repeating lines and phrases

> 'Now whether is this a rich man's house,
> Or whether is it a poor?'

such repetition lacked that addition of meaning, the forward
thrust of biblical parallelism echoed in Byron's

> Pale grew thy cheek and cold
> Colder thy kiss.
> Truly that hour foretold
> Sorrow to this.

And, as we shall see, the romantic poets themselves acknowledged that this incremental repetition was biblical in source.

Smart's *Song* is distinguished from contemporary verse not
only by the rhythms but also by the biblical simplicity both
of diction and imagery which ignores the traditional periphrases and 'decency' to create a wonderfully vivid effect.

> Strong is the lion—like a coal
> His eyeball—like a bastion's mole
>   His chest against the foes;
> Strong the gier-eagle on his sail,
> Strong against tide, th'enormous whale
>   Emerges as he goes.
>
> But stronger still, in earth and air,
> And in the sea, the man of pray'r,
>   And far beneath the tide:
> And in the seat to faith assign'd,
> Where ask is have, where seek is find,
>   Where knock is open wide.

The compression of the last two lines is typical of many
stanzas in the poem—that sense of urgency which skims over
the logical argument in a rush of feeling, leaving the reader to
supply, or rather to sense instinctively, the connections or
missing words. In the following passage from Job, for example,
the fact that it is God who provides the food for wild creatures
—which is the point at issue—is left for the reader to deduce:

Wilt thou hunt the prey for the lion? or fill the appetite of the
young lions when they couch in their dens and abide in the covert

to lie in wait? Who provideth for the raven his food? When his young ones cry unto God, they wander for lack of meat.

So, in Smart's *Song* the ideas tumble out one after the other with no logical links to develop the argument, though the meaning is clear nonetheless.

> Open and naked of offence,
> Man's made of mercy, soul, and sense;
> God arm'd the snail and wilk;
> Be good to him that pulls the plough;
> Due food and care, due rest allow
> For her that yields thee milk.

Despite its obscurity and complexity, the sincerity, which is the motive power, carries the poem along. Significantly, this biblical theme of kindness to animals, as creatures of God, this messianic view of the wolf that lies down with the lamb and the little child that leads them, finds its way into this poem and thence, perhaps, to Coleridge. Smart writes of King David:

> Beauteous, yes beauteous more than these
> The shepherd king upon his knees,
> For his momentous trust;
> With wish of infinite conceit,
> For man, beast, mute, the small and great,
> And prostrate dust to dust.

While Coleridge takes as his central theme for the *Ancient Mariner:*

> He prayeth best, who loveth best
> All things, both great and small;
> For the dear God who loveth us,
> He made and loveth all.

The Hymns for the Amusement of Children Smart composed in the tradition of Bunyan and Watts. The idea of the purity and innocence of children is too self-evident to be connected with any one source. Certainly the Bible is rich in pictures of childish innocence—the infant Samuel, the young David among the sheepfolds—but similar conceptions can be traced back to Locke and further to Plato. Wordsworth's concern with childhood is usually thought to be derived through

Hartley from Locke's *tabula rasa*, but it has been argued that he may well have inherited some part of it, through Vaughan, from the rabbinic writings on the subject which were attracting attention in the seventeenth century.[1] At all events, the tradition of poems for children was from Bunyan to Blake an essentially religious tradition and may well have contributed to Wordsworth's emphasis upon the unspoiled raptures of childhood.[2]

Apart from these hymns for children, Smart composed a collection of *Hymns and Spiritual Songs* for adults. They were filled with that spirit of humility before the divine throne which permeated the hymnology of Methodism and other nonconformist sects, eventually infiltrating into the hymns of the official Church itself.

> Words of endless adoration,
>   Christ I to thy call appear;
> On my knees in meek prostration
>   To begin a better year.[3]

Tucked away in one of these many hymns are two stanzas which serve to highlight that revolution in poetry which his *Jubilate Agno* and *Song to David* had marked—the rejection of neo-classical wit in favour of the devout rapture of the Bible. Hymn xi opens:

> Awake—arise—lift up thy voice,
>   Which as a trumpet swell,
> Rejoice in Christ—again rejoice,
>   And on his praises dwell.
>
> The muse at length, no more perplext
>   In search of human wit,
> Shall kneel her down, and take her text
>   From lore of sacred writ.

The voice of the poet is a trumpet-call spurning that human

---

[1] L. C. Martin, 'Henry Vaughan and the Theme of Infancy' in *Studies Presented to Sir Herbert Grierson* (Oxford, 1938), p. 243.

[2] This does not include the insipid verses of Ambrose Philips, addressed to children in a style more comprehensible to the fond parent. They earned him the nickname of 'Namby-Pamby'.   [3] *Hymn*, i.

wit, which in Smart's view had spoiled the poetry of an earlier generation.

Cowper, like Smart, in his earlier years remained close to the neo-classical tradition, translating many of his own poems into excellent Latin verse. A comparison of his *Poplar Field* with its Latin version reveals how dependent his English poetry was upon the nuances, rhythms and inversions of the classical tradition. But like such Christian predecessors as Jerome and Milton, his love for the classics was tempered by his contempt for classical paganism. For Cowper, the worship of Reason in the original Augustan age was its most serious failing, compared with the biblical tradition of humble faith. To his translation of Horace's *Odes* II, *x*, with its advocacy of the golden mean as the ideal for perfect living, Cowper attached his *Reflection on the Foregoing Ode* in which he felt compelled to reply:

> And is this all? Can Reason do no more
> Than bid me shun the deep and dread the shore?
> Sweet moralist! afloat on life's rough sea,
> The Christian has an art unknown to thee!
> He holds no parley with unmanly fears,
> Where duty bids he confidently steers,
> Faces a thousand dangers at her call,
> And, trusting in his God, surmounts them all.

It is strange to read this proud boast by one whose terrors drove him mad and who later used this same pathetic metaphor of a drowning man to describe his own sense of hopelessness; but during his quieter periods, it was this deep faith in God which kept him sane. At all events, Reason, he decided, was not for him, and in the realm of poetry he grew increasingly aware that the 'discipline' of contemporary verse had led to mere stereotype.

> Then Pope, as harmony itself exact,
> In verse, well disciplined, complete, compact . . .
> Made poetry a mere mechanic art,
> And every warbler has his tune by heart.[1]

As an antidote to this rationalized poetry, he looked back

---

[1] Cowper, *Table Talk*, 668.

longingly to the period when rules had not dominated verse composition. He writes of Eden, where poetry:

> Elegant as simplicity and warm
> As ecstasy, unmanacled by form,
> Not prompted, as in our degenerate days,
> By low ambition and the thirst for praise,
> Was natural, as is the flowing stream,
> And yet magnificent—a God the theme![1]

Ideally, he maintains, poetry's elegance should consist in its simplicity; it should be freed from the shackles of 'form', and the perfect theme for such ecstatic verse was God himself. It is an ideal totally at variance with the conventional verse of his day and, indeed, with the kind of verse which he was, at that period, writing himself. Similarly he states later in the same poem, but this time more explicitly, that the finest theme for poetry is religion and he condemns the staleness of contemporary verse.

> Pity! religion has so seldom found
> A skilful guide into poetic ground
> The flowers would spring where'er she deign'd
>   to stray,
> And every Muse attend her in her way . . .
> The shelves are full, all other themes are sped;
> Hackney'd and worn to the last flimsy thread . . .
> 'Twere new indeed to see a bard all fire
> Touch'd with a coal from heaven assume the lyre.

The final couplet, with its reference to Isaiah, the prophet touched in a vision with a burning coal from heaven, again identifies the poet with the prophet. The discovery of parallelism had finally confirmed the suspicion that the biblical prophets wrote in verse, and the advocacy of their verse as magnificent by any valid literary criterion had placed them high in the rank of poetic models. Parallel with the conception of the prophet as a sublime poet, the ballad movement, fostered by the biblical interest, had begun to idealize the ancient bard. The Homeric-type bard, writing of the glorious past, of gods and heroes, and—what is more—writing without

[1] Ibid., 588 and 716.

sophistication from among the common people, became a new symbol of noble, inspired poetry. It was inevitable that these two parallel concepts should fuse to form the composite image of the prophet-bard, which became the new ideal for the preromantics.

In Gray's Pindaric ode entitled *The Bard*, for example, the fictitious poet stands like Jeremiah lamenting the fall of Jerusalem with prophetic fire:

> Robed in the sable garb of woe
> With haggard eyes the Poet stood;
> (Loose his beard and hoary hair
> Streamed like a meteor to the troubled air)
> And with a Master's hand and Prophet's fire
> Struck the deep sorrows of his lyre.

In an age of didacticism in poetry, when, as the frequent apologies and defences of poetry from Sidney onwards indicate, there was a feeling that poetry needed to be justified, the conception of the poet as a prophet foretelling the future, denouncing abuse, and speaking the word of God was inspiring and elevating. Sidney could only gesture vaguely towards the *vates*, but now the romantic poet could identify himself fully with the prophetic tradition. When Wordsworth first recited to Coleridge part of his *Prelude*—a poem dealing with the comparatively prosaic theme of the development of a poet's philosophy and art—Coleridge responded with particular praise for the prophetic quality of the work:

> Into my heart have I received that lay
> More than historic, that prophetic lay
> Wherein (high theme, by thee first sung aright)
> Of the foundations and the building up
> Of a human spirit thou hast dared to tell
> What may be told, to the understanding mind
> Revealable; and what within the mind
> By vital breathings secret as the soul
> Of vernal growth, oft quickens in the heart
> Thoughts all too deep for words!

Poetry had become what Wordsworth called 'the holy life of music and of verse', a lofty and at times sacred form of art, revealing to man the inner workings of his soul, and no longer needing to be elevated above mere 'amusement' by a display of classical erudition.

It was this new respect for the prophetic poet which prompted Goldsmith in his *Oratorio* (1764) to describe the figure of the prophet-bard as filled with awful rapture and the solemnity of the divine message:

> But hold! see foremost of the captive choir
> The master prophet grasps the full-toned lyre.
> Mark where he sits with executing art,
> Feels for each tone, and speeds it to the heart;
> See how prophetic rapture fills his form,
> Awful as clouds that nurse the growing storm.

and Burns wrote in *The Cotter's Saturday Night* of the father reading to his family from '. . . rapt Isaiah's wild seraphic fire'. Again the prophet is associated with fire and with this in mind we can appreciate more fully the significance of Cowper's longing to see

> . . . a bard all fire
> Touch'd with a coal from heaven assume the lyre.

In his *Olney Hymns* Cowper followed his own advice by guiding Religion into poetic ground, and the gentle piety and desperate longing for perfect unshakable faith expressed themselves in personal, simple and yet profoundly emotional poems, abounding in biblical allusions and paraphrases. The Methodist hymns, however direct may be their relation of individual experience and feeling, were intended primarily for public singing and written with an eye to the singer; but Cowper's hymns were intended, one feels, only for himself and his God. The first hymn is typical of that personal quality which permeates the entire collection.

> Oh! for a closer walk with God;
> A calm and heavenly frame;
> A light to shine upon the road
> That leads me to the Lamb!
>
> Where is the blessedness I knew
> When first I saw the Lord?

Where is the soul-refreshing view
Of Jesus and his word?

What peaceful hours I once enjoy'd!
How sweet their memory still!
But they have left an aching void,
The world can never fill.

There is no attempt here to clothe emotion in mythological form or to blunt it by periphrases. The sadness and hope are related simply and movingly. In fact the imagery of the hymns as a whole is elemental, being drawn like that of the Bible from the natural world.

I was a grovelling creature once,
And basely cleaved to earth;
I wanted spirit to renounce
The clod that gave me birth.

But God has breathed upon a worm,
And sent me from above
Wings such as clothe an angel's form,
The wings of joy and love.

Outside these specifically religious poems, much of his verse remained classical in form. Yet even there an intensely personal note entered occasionally, and in *The Castaway*, the most moving of all his poems, the final stanza throbs with dread.

No voice divine the storm allayed
No light propitious shone,
When snatch'd from all effectual aid
We perish'd each alone.
But I beneath a rougher sea,
And whelm'd in deeper gulfs than he.

The individualism of the poem, the simplicity of its imagery, the hymnal form and, not least, the allusion to the Psalmist's call for divine aid from the deeps which engulf are all symptomatic of those changes in poetry wrought during the century.

Blake is, of course, the prophet-poet *par excellence* of English literature, filled as he was with the conviction that

159

poetry has no function to perform other than to transmit to mankind the Word of God, to correct human backsliding, and to offer a vision of the spiritual world beyond reality. It requires no critical insight to discern his debt to the prophetic tradition—and yet there is room for an important corrective to the prevalent view. Only too frequently critics write of Blake as though his was a sudden, almost inexplicable eruption of intensely individualistic poetry which happened to employ, among other models, the idiom of the Old Testament. In fact, so far from merely adopting biblical idiom as a suitable means of expression, Blake found in the Old Testament the very source of his inspiration, deriving from it his concept of the poet as a fiery visionary seeing the eternal in the transitory, and rejecting mere social expediency in favour of justice, mercy, and compassion. He forms, indeed, the culmination of that concern with the visionary power and ethical insistence of Hebrew poetry which has formed the subject of these chapters.

So much has been written on this extraordinarily complex, contradictory figure that almost any statement about him has to bristle with modifications and reservations. The Old Testament Jehovah he detested as the embodiment of bloodthirsty tyranny, and contemporary Christianity was for him a perversion of the true religion. Yet (and here we are in the midst of a typically Blakean paradox) the Bible, including the Old Testament, was the noblest and most inspired literature in the world, and the spirit of Hebrew prophecy permeated not merely Blake's verse but even his daily life. He saw the world around him, the industrialization of England, the oppression of the poor, the ugliness and squalor of the towns, through the eyes of the biblical prophet. Himself he regarded as the bearer of the divine message, and in him the traditions of the ancient bard and the Hebrew prophet met and mingled as we have seen them mingle in such fictitious characters as Gray's *Bard*. In place of the conventional invocation to the classical muse, Blake solemnly warns his readers to heed the divine message— the message, in fact, of the prophet-bard.

160

Hear the voice of the Bard!
Who Present, Past, & Future, sees;
Whose ears have heard
The Holy Word
That walk'd among the ancient trees.

The emphasis here is upon *ancient*. God, to Blake, is the
Ancient of Days. The ancient trees, reminiscent of Eden in
which God walked in the cool of the day, form the background to the biblical picture. It is a form of primitivism in
which the traditions of the Bible occupy the most honoured
place. It had by now become almost commonplace to class
biblical poetry with such 'primitive' writings as those of
Homer and the ancient Celts, but no one before Blake (and
perhaps no one after) had taken the primitivist interpretation
quite so far. For him, the pre-Abrahamic period of the Bible—
the period of Adam and Noah—became identified with the
Druidic civilization at the peak of its development, before it
declined to that level at which it was remembered by subsequent generations. The binding of Isaac thus constituted the
Bible's formal rejection of those human sacrifices performed
on the Druidic altar. In Blake's prophetic books, the two
civilizations become inextricably intertwined, and over a
drawing of a massive trilithon from Stonehenge published in
his *Milton* appear the lines

When shall Jerusalem return & overspread all the Nations?
Return! return to Lambeth's Vale, O building of human souls!
Thence stony Druid Temples overspread the Island white
And thence from Jerusalem's ruins, from her walls of salvation
And praise: thro' the whole Earth were rear'd. . . .

Blake's insistence on this 'Druidic' element in biblical
poetry strengthened the growing prophet-bard identification
and became part of his own belief that the stylized verse of
his age had lost contact with the natural well-springs of true
poetry. In an early poem, *To the Muses*, he announced in
effect his new poetic manifesto—his determination to revive
the almost-forgotten modes of ancient bardic poetry:

Whether on chrystal rocks ye rove,
Beneath the bosom of the sea

161

Wand'ring in many a coral grove;
Fair Nine, forsaking Poetry!

How have you left the antient love
The bards of old enjoy'd in you!
The languid strings do scarcely move!
The sound is forc'd, the notes are few!

The restraint and sophistication of Greece and Rome formed for him the very antithesis of the fervour of the Bible, and throughout his writings he was bitterly opposed to their contemporary domination of the arts.

Greece and Rome, as Babylon and Egypt, so far from being parents of Arts and Sciences as they pretend, were destroyers of all Art.[1]

The classics he rejected out of hand, claiming instead:

The Old and New Testament are the Great Code of Art.

Such a declaration marks the collapse of the classics as the supreme arbiter of taste and the broadening of literary and artistic standards to include those of other lands and other times, the standards of the Bible prominent among them.

In the *Songs of Innocence*, the results of the change in model are not so apparent as they were to be in his later works. The songs are not biblical in their metrical form, although, by dispensing with the periphrases, the wit, and the decorum of Augustan verse and adopting in their stead the directness of scriptural imagery, they achieve a freshness and lightness which immediately distinguish them from the more ponderous forms of contemporary verse. The pastoral scene no longer depicts a Corydon sporting with an Amaryllis, but a shepherd guarding his flock, symbolic of God protecting the innocent—in fact, Psalm xxiii not paraphrased but turned into a new poem.

How sweet is the Shepherd's sweet lot!
From the morn to the evening he strays;

[1] Blake, *Poetry and Prose*, ed. G. Keynes (London, 1943), p. 583. All subsequent quotations are from the same edition. For Blake's attitude to the Old Testament, see N. Frye, *Fearful Symmetry* (Princeton, 1958), pp. 108 f.

He shall follow the sheep all the day,
And his tongue shall be filled with praise.

For he hears the lamb's innocent call;
And he hears the ewe's tender reply;
He is watchful while they are in peace,
For they know when their Shepherd is nigh.

Technically it is not a religious poem, but so replete is it with biblical allusions and symbols that its effect is profoundly religious nonetheless. Yet even when there are no symbols and no biblical echoes to point to the source, the biblical ethos is still apparent. The *Laughing Song* has no direct allusion to scriptural passages, yet its rippling laughter is expressed as nature and all that is in it bursting out into song—a song reminiscent of the Psalmist's paean to God: 'Let the heavens rejoice and let the earth be glad; let the sea roar and the fulness thereof. Let the field be joyful and all that is in it.'

When the green woods laugh with the voice of joy,
And the dimpling stream runs laughing by;
When the air does laugh with our merry wit,
And the green hill laughs with the noise of it.

In the *Songs of Experience*, the biblical content is more striking, and a note of high seriousness has replaced the joy of the earlier poems. The concept of the prophet bearing the heavy burden of his holy message predominates, and the symbols of thorns, sheep, plagues, and harlots are used with the same vividness as in the Bible.

But most thro' midnight streets I hear
How the youthful Harlot's curse
Blasts the new born Infant's tear,
And blights with plagues the Marriage hearse.

The solemn word-play of (*t*)*ear* and the ironic perception that the same vehicle serves both as wedding-carriage and as hearse is far removed from the conscious wit of neo-classicism. On Belinda's dressing-table in the *Rape of Lock* we are told.

The Tortoise here and Elephant unite.

The humour lies in the apparent absurdity concealing what is perfectly reasonable—a comb made of ivory and tortoise-shell. Blake, however, is, like the biblical prophet, concerned with a far graver irony of which the initial incongruity is symbolic—the perversion of the natural, divine order in which marriage should lead to fruitfulness and multiplying instead of disease and death. Or to put it more simply, the neo-classicist is concerned ultimately with the harmony of the universe, while the prophet sees the disharmony and longs to rectify it.

The most powerful of all these songs, the *Tyger*, uses the same technique as the leviathan passage in Job. Question after question is thrust home to contrast the insignificance of man with the omnipotence of God, and the poem again skims over the logical connections as the excitement of the passage sweeps it forward. But in Blake's poem there is, in addition, the wondering humility of Job himself:

> What the hammer? what the chain?
> In what furnace was thy brain?
> What the anvil? what dread grasp
> Dare its deadly terrors clasp?

It is this very humility before the glories of creation, this sense of wonder at nature which, perhaps more than anything else, divides the romantic from the neo-classicist. And it is a sense of wonder which stems directly from the Psalms of David.

> To see a World in a Grain of Sand,
> And a Heaven in a Wild Flower,
> Hold Infinity in the palm of your hand
> And Eternity in an hour.

It recalls such passages as Psalm xix where, without speech or sound, the works of creation declare the glory of God.

Blake did not study the Bible in Hebrew until late in life, but he was, of course, steeped in the cadences and idioms of the Authorized Version. In his first publication, *Poetical Sketches*, Blake inserted some prose passages, among them the *Couch of Death*, in which the parallelism, the idioms, and even the thoughts themselves come straight from the Bible.

My hand is feeble, how should I stretch it out? My ways are sinful, how should I raise mine eyes? My voice hath used deceit, how should I call on Him who is Truth? My breath is loathsome, how should he not be offended? If I lay my face in the dust, the grave opens its mouth for me: if I lift up my head, sin covers me as a cloak![1]

The last verses are a reworking of Psalm cxxxix: 'If I ascend up into heaven, thou art there; if I make my bed in hell, behold thou art there', but they are not a paraphrase. He has not tried to turn the biblical original into contemporary verse. On the contrary, he has created something new by immersing himself in the world of the Bible and recreating from within. The result is, in a way, original biblical writing, the style being recaptured after a lapse of hundreds of years.

To read modern critics discussing the metres of Blake's prophetic books is to find oneself back in the seventeenth-century examination of biblical poetry before the discovery of parallelism. One eminent Blakean scholar writes of the *Song of Liberty*: 'It is really alexandrines with regular caesuras, but with a foot that varies from anapest to dactyl, with inter-polated iambs and trochees. . . . To read these metrically, great violence must be done to the normal accent of the words.' He admits at the end of the chapter that '. . . at some moments [Blake] seems to have reached a complete liberation from metre in favour of the cadence.'[2]

In fact, Blake had simply adopted the biblical parallelist forms which ignore regular metre and rely instead upon a rhythm of meaning. By including the *Couch of Death* in his *Poetical Sketches*, Blake had shown that he regarded it as poetry even when it was set out as prose. In the prophetic books, however, Blake, like Smart before him, set out his parallelist writing line by line in much the same way as Lowth had set out his own translation of Isaiah. In the introduction to *Jerusalem*, Blake explained more fully his rejection of a conventional, regular metre in favour of a rhythm dictated solely by the sense of the passage:

[1] *The Couch of Death*, p. 42.
[2] S. Foster Damon, *William Blake: his philosophy and symbols* (Gloucester, Mass., 1958), pp. 57, 58 and 61.

When this Verse was first dictated to me, I consider'd a Monotonous Cadence, like that used by Milton & Shakespeare & all
Writers of English Blank Verse, derived from the modern bondage
of Rhyming, to be a necessary and indispensible part of Verse. But
I soon found that in the mouth of a true Orator such monotony
was not only awkward, but as much a bondage as rhyme itself. I
therefore have produced a variety in every line, both of cadence &
number of syllables. Every word and every letter is studied and
put into its fit place; the terrific numbers are reserved for the
terrific parts, the mild & gentle for the mild & gentle parts, and
the prosaic for the inferior parts; all are necessary to each other.
Poetry Fetter'd Fetters the Human Race.

Despite the attempts of critics, the 'unfetter'd' verse which
follows will not yield to analysis into metrical feet, for its
rhythms are sense-rhythms pulsating in time with the meaning.

> I am not a God afar off, I am a brother and friend:
> Within your bosoms I reside, and you reside in me:
> Lo! we are One, forgiving all Evil, Not seeking recompense.
> Ye are my members, O ye sleepers of Beulah, land of shades!

Not all of the prophetic writings slip so easily into parallelist
forms—often he breaks away even from this sense-rhythm in
order to create a rolling, oratorical movement, but parallelism
forms the unifying metre of these later books. A significant
advance from Smart's parallelism is that whereas the latter
models his verse only on the Psalms, Blake turns from hallelujahs to the prophetic denunciation of social oppression,
borrowing from the prophets the imagery of chains, darkness,
lions and wolves.

> Let the slave grinding in the mill run out into the field,
> Let him look up into the heavens & laugh in the bright air;
> Let the inchained soul, shut up in darkness and in sighing,
> Whose face has never seen a smile in thirty weary years,
> Rise and look out; his chains are loose, his dungeon doors
>   are open;
> And let his wife and children return from the oppressor's
>   scourge.
> They look behind at every step, & believe it is a dream,
> Singing: 'The Sun has left its blackness & has found a
>   fresher morning,
> 'And the fair Morn rejoices in the clear & cloudless night;

166

'For Empire is no more, and now the Lion & Wolf shall cease.'[1]

So complete is Blake's imaginative transference to the biblical scene that the world around him appears in a double-focus, the biblical being superimposed upon the real world.

Medway mingled with Kishon; Thames reciev'd the heavenly Jordan.

and the names of the prophetic books—*Jerusalem, Ahania, Urizen, Thel*—if not actually biblical, sound as if they ought to be. The real world existed for him only as a stepping-stone to eternity.

'What,' it will be Question'd, 'When the Sun rises, do you not see a round disk of fire somewhat like a Guinea?' O no, no, I see an Innumerable company of the Heavenly host crying, 'Holy, Holy, Holy is the Lord God Almighty.' I question not my Corporeal or Vegetative Eye any more than I would Question a Window concerning a Sight. I look thro' it and not with it.[2]

This passage marks a reversal of Selden's empirical approach, his rejection of biblical allegorizing on the grounds that a close scrutiny of the facts would prove more fruitful. Yet Blake has not returned to medieval allegory with all its typological reading of the Old Testament. The Bible was still to be read as true history, but was to be seen also as opening a window on to the world of eternal values.

True, Platonic philosophy had conceived of a similar dichotomy between the visible and the ideal world, but Blake repudiated Plato—'The Gods of Greece and Egypt were Mathematical Diagrams—See Plato's Works'[3]—and he regarded the Bible as the exclusive source of his dual vision. Jerusalem and England merge into one, as do past and present, so that in one of his most famous poems he waits on England's hillsides for Elijah's chariot to descend from heaven and equip him for battle against the spiritual darkness of England.

> And did the Countenance Divine
> Shine forth upon our clouded hills?

[1] *America*, p. 203, and *Jerusalem*, p. 539.
[2] *A Vision of the Last Judgment*, p. 652.
[3] Engraving on the *Laocoon Group*, p. 581.

And was Jerusalem builded here
Among these dark Satanic Mills?

Bring me my Bow of burning gold:
Bring me my Arrows of desire:
Bring me my Spear: O clouds unfold!
Bring me my Chariot of fire.

At times his castigation of the enemy and his lament for the
calamities which have befallen Albion are expressed in such
biblical terms that they are almost indistinguishable from the
original. The following passage might have come straight
from the Bible:

My tents are fall'n! my pillars are in ruins! my children dash'd
Upon Egypt's iron floors & the marble pavements of Assyria!
I melt my soul in reasoning amongst the towers of Heshbon.
Mount Zion is a cruel rock, & no more dew
Nor rain, no more the spring of the rock appears, but cold
Hard and obdurate are the furrows of the mountain of wine
     & oil.[1]

This 'double-focus' extends to his use of imagery which he
borrowed directly from the Bible and which, for the most
part, meant little to an Englishman outside the context of the
Bible itself. The wine, oil, tents and deserts were vivid metaphors in Blake's verse despite the fact that neither he nor
most of his readers had ever seen an olive growing on a tree
or a tent spread in a wilderness. They were vivid because both
he and his reader knew of them through the Bible, had learnt
of them in their childhood and associated them with religious
purity, moral vision and divine presence. It was by applying
them to the real world about him that Blake drove home his
message and, as it were, revived the Bible by reliving it in
a modern age.

In his verse there is the Hebraic swiftness of thrust behind
each image and the same quick change from one apt image to
another.

He drinks thee up like water, like wine he pours thee
Into his tuns: thy Daughters are trodden in his vintage.

[1] *Jerusalem*, p. 539.

He makes thy Sons the trampling of his bulls, they are
    plow'd
And harrow'd for his profit.[1]

There is no avoidance here of 'mean' and 'vulgar' metaphors.
Each simile is drawn deliberately from the most common
and prosaic scenes and the maximum power extracted from
each to add force to the divine message. The sophisticated
detachment of neo-classical poetry has been replaced by an
urgent concern with justice and righteousness, with a denunciation of moral wrong before which all must give way. Although
its biblical quality is imitative, it produces a greater sense of
immediacy than the more relaxed and consciously artistic
poetry which the previous generation had cultivated. And
lest we forget the contrast such poetry afforded with the
Augustan, we may recall Pope's lines:

> Ye shady beeches, and ye cooling streams,
> Defence from Phoebus', not from Cupid's beams,
> To you I mourn, nor to the deaf I sing,
> 'The woods shall answer and their echo ring.'
> The hills and rocks attend my doleful lay;
> Why art thou prouder and more hard than they?
> The bleating sheep with my complaints agree,
> They parched with heat, and I inflam'd by thee.
> The sultry Sirius burns the thirsty plains,
> While in my heart, eternal winter reigns.

We are conscious throughout of the stylized classical word
order, with the central caesura acting as pivot for the witty
balance and contrasts, the classical allusions to Phoebus and
Cupid, which serve at the same time as poetic periphrases, and
the quotation from Spenser for the benefit of the well-read.
But above all, the poem emerges as a literary exercise, a
formal composition for a polite age, devoid of any real emotion.

Blake writes on a similar theme:

> I will call; & who shall answer me? I will sing; who shall reply?
> For from my pleasant hills behold the living, living springs.
> Running among my green pastures, delighting among my trees.
> I am not here alone: my flocks, you are my brethren;
> And you birds that sing & adorn the sky, you are my sisters.

[1] Ibid., p. 438.

I sing, & you reply to my song: I rejoice, & you are glad.
Follow me, O my flocks; we will now descend into the valley.
O how delicious are the grapes, flourishing in the sun!
How clear the spring of the rock, running among the golden
  sand![1]

The metre is created by the emotional content which, now flowing smoothly, now swirling around a thought, creates with its sudden spurts and pauses the loosely constructed rhythms of the poem, providing a pulsating undercurrent to the feeling. The setting is oriental with its golden sands, delicious grapes, and bright sun, and yet the poet has transferred himself emotionally to the setting, feeling the warmth, drinking in every detail of the scene and delighting in its beauty. Between him and the natural world there is a bond; the sheep are his brethren, the birds his sisters, and the biblical echoes from the *Song of Songs* help to unify the whole picture as one of peace on earth under the beneficent eye of God. It is a far cry from the conventional pastoral of Pope and a clear augury of romanticism.

On the Continent, the Ossianic poems, themselves fostered by the new admiration for biblical poetry, had a deep and lasting effect on French and German writers alike; but even there it remained closely connected with the biblical movement. Goethe, who was so impressed by the works of Macpherson, first learned of them in his youth through Herder, and in recording this fateful meeting Goethe placed first among the literary innovations to which Herder had introduced him the new interest in the ancient poetry of the Hebrews. On the basis of this new emotional interpretation of parallelism, he tried his own hand at a translation of the *Song of Songs*, describing it as 'the most magnificent collection of love songs which God ever created.' Nor could he have found a better guide than Herder; for the latter soon combined his wide knowledge of the Bible with his romantic interests to produce a remarkably fine sequel to Lowth's lectures entitled the *Spirit of Hebrew Poetry*. In this, he

[1] Pope, *Summer: the Second Pastoral*, 13, and Blake, *Vala or the Four Zoas*, p. 359.

[2] L. Lewisohn, *Goethe* (New York, 1949), i, 52 and 126.

developed Lowth's more scholarly presentation of the theory of parallelism into a lyrical eulogy of biblical poetry, treating it as a worthy model for romantic verse:

So soon as the heart gives way to its emotions, wave follows upon wave, and that is parallelism. The heart is never exhausted, it has forever something new to say. So soon as the first wave has passed away, or broken itself upon the rocks, the second swells again and returns as before. This pulsating of nature, this breathing of emotion, appears in all the language of passion, and would you not have that in poetry which is most clearly the offspring of emotion?[1]

(II)

This passage from Herder may be regarded as the climax of the movement we have been tracing. That scholarly enquiry into the Bible, which had given the original impetus to an investigation of its metrical forms and of the primitive rites on which its imagery was based, had been swept aside by the realization that it contained an essentially new type of poetry—new insofar as the Western world had ignored it as a poetic model until now. In an age assuming as unquestionable the pre-eminence of classical poetry over all other models, the discovery that the Holy Bible achieved its poetic effects by 'waves' of emotional rhythms broke the monopolistic authority of neo-classical form, sounding the knell of those neatly balanced couplets of which Keats wrote so disparagingly:

> with a puling infant's force
> They swayed about upon a rocking horse,
> And thought it Pegasus . . . ye were dead
> To things ye knew not of,—were closely wed
> To musty laws lined out with wretched rule
> And compass vile: so that ye taught a school
> Of dolts to smooth, inlay, and clip, and fit,
> Till like the certain wands of Jacob's wit,
> Their verses tallied.[2]

But as we move from the preromantic school to the romantic, we must not make the mistake of expecting that same

---

[1] J. G. Herder, *The Spirit of Hebrew Poetry*, tr. J. Marsh (London, 1833), i, 41. [2] *Sleep and Poetry*, 185 f.

wholehearted immersion in biblical idiom and thought as we have seen in Smart and Blake. If the Bible had served as a gateway through which the preromantic could escape from the strict rules of Augustan poetry, once outside he was free to experiment with new forms. Indeed, one of the hallmarks of romanticism is its insistence upon original creativity rather than the slavish imitation of ancient masters, and if the romantics did look to Spenser, Shakespeare, the balladists, and a host of other writers for inspiration, they demanded complete freedom to select from a variety of models. Among those models, the Bible still held a highly respected place, but it had, in a sense, served its turn, and it is to be discerned as a submerged current rather than as a mainstream in the writings of the romantic school itself.

What is particularly significant, however, is the readiness with which the romantic poets acknowledged their debt to biblical forms even when the reader can perceive only the faintest resemblance. For it confirms that however freely the poet might be writing, he was conscious that his own youthful acquaintance with biblical poetry and the realization in those impressionable years that it constituted a new poetic model had provided an impetus for his own experimentation. Wordsworth, for example, in one of his early and less successful poems, *The Thorn*, experimented with incremental repetition —a device used with extraordinary effect throughout the whole body of romantic poetry, and most notably in Coleridge's *Ancient Mariner*. *The Thorn* contains no visible trace of biblical form, a typical stanza running:

> Now wherefore, thus, by day and night,
> In rain, in tempest and in snow,
> Thus to the dreary mountain top
> Does this poor woman go?
> And why sits she beside the Thorn
> When the blue daylight's in the sky
> Or when the whirlwind's on the hill,
> Or frosty air is keen and still,
> And wherefore does she cry?—
> O wherefore? wherefore? tell me why
> Does she repeat that doleful cry?

Yet in a lengthy note attached to the poem and intended to 'excuse' the apparent tautologies, Wordsworth pointed to biblical parallelism as the primary source of this incremental repetition. The reader, he insists, cannot be too often reminded that Poetry is passion, and that passion makes a man 'cling to the same words, or words of the same character' so that such apparent tautology is frequently extremely beautiful. He concludes:

. . . from a spirit of fondness, exultation, and gratitude, the mind luxuriates in the repetition of words which appear successfully to communicate its feelings. The truth of these remarks might be shown by innumerable passages from the Bible, and from the impassioned poetry of every nation. 'Awake, awake, Deborah! &c. Judges, chap. v, verses 12th, 27th, and part of 28th. See also the whole of that tumultuous and wonderful Poem.

If, therefore, romantic poetry is not so patently indebted to the Bible as the writings of Smart and Blake, it was still drawing much of its sustenance and vigour from the more general inspiration which the Scriptures had afforded; and behind even so secular a poem as *The Thorn* lay the pulsating rhythms of 'Awake, awake, Deborah: awake, awake, utter a song: arise, Barak, and lead thy captivity captive, thou son of Abinoam.'

The only romantic poet capable of reading the Old Testament in the original was Coleridge, who described himself as a 'tolerable Hebraist', and in fact translated 'A Hebrew Dirge; chanted in the Great Synagogue, St. James's Place, Aldgate', publishing it as *Israel's Lament*. In his later years he summarized his entire life's work as having been an attempt to reconcile the Hebraic and Greek modes of thought.[1] The majority of these attempts were, of course, concerned with his Unitarian beliefs and hence theological in nature, but they were interestingly reflected in his poetic theories. Basically he was concerned with the contrast between the artificial, literary devices employed in classical poetry and the more

[1] See J. B. Beer, *Coleridge the Visionary* (London, 1959), p. 306, note 33. Coleridge had read Lowth's work on Hebrew poetry, as is recorded in G. Whalley, 'The Bristol Library Borrowings of Southey and Coleridge, 1793–8', *The Library*, 5th series, iv, 123, No. 84.

vivid directness of Hebrew poetry—in fact, a contrast remarkably close to that which has formed the central theme of this present work.

In the opening chapter of his *Biographia Literaria*, Coleridge recorded with gratitude the important lesson he had learned from his schoolmaster—that same schoolmaster, incidentally, who had taught him Hebrew. The Latinisms with which pupils at that period sprinkled their verse-writing his teacher rejected with scorn.

> *Lute, harp,* and *lyre, Muse, Muses,* and *inspirations, Pegasus, Parnassus,* and *Hippocrene* were all an abomination to him. In fancy I can almost hear him now, exclaiming 'Harp? Harp? Lyre? Pen and ink, boy, you mean! Pierian spring? Oh, aye! The cloister-pump, I suppose!'

From this early warning against classical euphemisms and periphrases in poetry, Coleridge later developed his distaste for neo-classical verse. While not blind to the merits of Pope and his followers, he argued that their writings were in fact 'translations of prose thoughts into poetic language', and he perceived that the source of this prosaic quality was their training in Latin versification, their use of the *Gradus* to fill 'halves and quarters of lines'. Elsewhere, in a passage central to his theory of poetry, his well-known distinction between *fancy* and *imagination,* he suggested that the antipole to classical mythologizing (which constitutes a major portion of those periphrases his schoolmaster had condemned) was to be found in the vitality of Hebrew poetry. In ancient Greece, he maintains:

> All natural objects were *dead,* mere hollow statues, but there was a Godkin or Goddessling *included* in each. . . . At best it is but fancy, or the aggregating faculty of the mind, not imagination or the modifying and coadunating faculty. This the Hebrew poets appear to me to have possessed beyond all others, and next to them the English. In the Hebrew poets each thing has a life of its own, and yet they are all our life.[1]

Although this plea for the demythologizing of poetry was ostensibly directed against the Greeks, it occurs in a letter

[1] Letter to W. Sotheby, 10 September 1802.

discussing the dull nature-imagery employed by most of his contemporaries who used such classical mythology as a background decoration for their verse. Again, therefore, Hebrew poetry is offered as an antidote to the classical influence on contemporary verse.

This reference to biblical poetry was far from casual, and time after time Coleridge returned to the Bible as a standard whereby to check the validity of his definitions. In a philosophical enquiry into the nature of poetry, for example, he reaches the conclusion: 'The final definition then, so deduced, may be thus worded. A poem is that species of composition, which is opposed to works of science, by proposing for its *immediate* object pleasure, not truth.' A few lines later, however, he recalls that 'The first chapter of Isaiah —(indeed a very large portion of the whole book)—is poetry in the most emphatic sense; yet it would be not less irrational than strange to assert, that pleasure, and not truth was the immediate object of the prophet.' Consequently, he finds it necessary to modify his original definition to read: 'The poet described in ideal perfection, brings the whole soul of man into activity.'[1] The change is fundamental; for the original 'pleasure' definition is more applicable to the Augustan concept of poetry as an amusement, whereas the final form insists upon the *soul*, with all its biblical and romantic associations.

This concern with Hebraism in the critical writings finds its counterpart in Coleridge the poet. His well-known reply to the precursors of Higher Criticism—'Whatever *finds* me, bears witness for itself that it has proceeded from a Holy Spirit'— presupposed that the Bible was not, as so many of the rationalist preachers of the age had argued, a body of reasoned belief, but a source of personal inspiration appealing to the heart rather than the mind. In the lines immediately preceding this statement, he relates how in the Bible

I have found words for my inmost thoughts, songs for my joy, utterances for my hidden griefs, and pleadings for my shame and my feebleness.

He read the Scriptures, soaking himself in their idioms until

[1] *Biographia Literaria*, chapter xlv.

their songs of joy became *his* songs of joy, and he writes of the Psalmist as

. . . the royal Harper, to whom I have so often submitted myself as a *many-stringed instrument* for his fire-tipt fingers to traverse, while every several nerve of emotion, passion, thought, that thrids the flesh-and-blood of our common humanity, responded to the touch.[1]

It was impossible that a poet should so attune himself to the Bible without catching something of its timbre and in the following passage, for example, the verse cuts across line division, almost spurning the metre as it throbs with a rhythm of meaning:

> Oh! let not English women drag their flight
> Fainting beneath the burthen of their babes,
> Of the sweet infants, that but yesterday
> Laughed at the breast! Sons, brothers, husbands, all
> Who ever gazed with fondness on the forms
> Which grew up with you round the same fireside,
> And all who ever heard the sabbath-bells
> Without the infidels scorn, make yourselves pure![2]

Here the source is clearly the prophetic books, with their protest against oppression and injustice; but elsewhere he turned to the 'royal Harper' for that animation of nature in which all the beauties of the world join in unison to praise the Creator:

> Motionless torrents! silent cataracts!
> Who made you glorious as the Gates of Heaven
> Beneath the keen full moon? Who bade the sun
> Clothe you with rainbows? Who, with living flowers
> Of loveliest blue, spread garlands at your feet?—
> God! let the torrents, like a shout of nations,
> Answer! and let the ice-plains echo, God!
> God! sing ye meadow-streams with gladsome voice!
> Ye pine groves, with your soft and soul-like sounds!
> And they too have a voice, yon piles of snow,
> And in their perilous fall shall thunder, God![3]

The sublime cataracts and torrents still inspire the poet with

---

[1] *Confessions of an Inquiring Spirit*, Letters i and iii.
[2] *Fears in Solitude*, 132–9.   [3] *Hymn Before Sunrise*, 53 f.

a specifically religious awe, and serve as an affirmation of faith in the moral purpose of the universe. Indeed, of all the romantic poets, Coleridge's concept of God is the least Deistic and the closest to that of the Bible. When he does veer towards Deism, he stops short, administering to himself a sharp rap over the knuckles. In *The Aeolian Harp*, he toys with the idea that perhaps all animated nature consists merely of

> organic harps diversely framed,
> That tremble into thoughts, as o'er them sweeps
> Plastic and vast, one intellectual breeze,
> At once the Soul of each, and God of all?

But at once he perceives Sara's disapproval of such unhallowed thoughts, and admits that she is right to reprimand him.

> Well hast thou said and holily dispraised
> These shapings of the unregenerated mind;
> Bubbles that glitter as they rise and break
> On vain Philosophy's ay-bubbling spring.
> For never guiltless may I speak of him,
> The Incomprehensible! save when with awe
> I praise him, and with Faith that inly feels.

Perhaps most interesting of all is the incident which occurred in 1798, when he and Wordsworth were engaged in writing the *Lyrical Ballads* which was to inaugurate the new school of poetry. One day, Coleridge relates, they decided to amuse themselves by composing a 'Gothic' piece in the style of Salamon Gessner's *Death of Abel*, each of them writing one canto, the third to be composed by the person who finished first. Gessner's work, published before the Ossianic poems, was a somewhat turgid prose piece in no way indebted to the Bible linguistically; but in Coleridge's version, entitled *The Wanderings of Cain*, the parallelistic prose is unmistakably Jobian:

O that a man might live without the breath of his nostrils. So I might abide in darkness and blackness and an empty space! Yea, I would lie down, I would not rise, neither would I stir my limbs till I became as the rock in the den of the lion, on which the young lion resteth his head whilst he sleepeth. For the torrent that roareth far off hath a voice: and the clouds in heaven look terribly on me; the Mighty One who is against me speaketh in the wind of the cedar grove; and in silence am I dried up.

Coleridge won the competition because, as he generously put it, Wordsworth's taste was too austerely pure and simple for Gothic writing, and the work was never completed.

This unfinished prose-poem might have been no more than a literary oddity, were it not that his account of the incident ends with the phrase '. . . and the Ancient Mariner was written instead'. The Cain passage, then, was written while Coleridge was contemplating and perhaps even composing the *Ancient Mariner* with its submerged theme of the Wandering Jew who, like the Wandering Cain, is doomed to bear in eternal exile the heavy burden of his guilt.[1] In both, this haunting sense of guilt predominates; in both, there is a profound sense of divine justice and mercy; and in both, nature serves as the emissary of God's will. Cain hears in the natural world around him the angry voice of heaven just as the Mariner recognizes in the glorious yet bloody sun the symbol of 'God's own head' exacting retribution for sin.

And Cain lifted up his voice and cried bitterly, and said,'The Mighty One that persecuteth me is on this side and on that; he pursueth my soul like the wind, like the sandblast he passeth through me; he is around me even as the air!'

Again, like the Ancient Mariner, the lesson Cain has to learn is that of human love, and the prose-poem ends with the ghost of Abel answering sadly: ' "O that thou hadst had pity on me as I will have pity on thee. Follow me, Son of Adam! and bring thy child with thee!" And they three passed over the white sands between the rocks, silent as the shadows.'

The legend of the Wandering Jew was, of course, medieval in origin, but for the romantics he became partially identified with the biblical prophet, bearing the burden of his divine message and, like Jonah, unable to escape his onerous task. We have already seen how the prophet was identified with fire, and a famous passage from Jeremiah relates how the

[1] See J. B. Beer, op. cit., p. 145, for recent evidence that Coleridge himself thought of the Mariner as 'the everlasting Wandering Jew'.

178

prophet longed to be relieved of his wearisome duty: 'Then I said, I will not make mention of Him, nor speak any more in His name. But His word was in my heart as a burning fire shut up in my bones' (Jeremiah xx, 9).

So it is with the Ancient Mariner:

> Since then, at an uncertain hour,
> That agony returns:
> And till my ghastly tale is told,
> This heart within me burns.
>
> I pass, like night, from land to land;
> I have strange power of speech;
> That moment that his face I see,
> I know the man that must hear me:
> To him my tale I teach.

For all the ghastliness of the tale, the message he brings is one of love for God's creatures, and the knowledge that

> the dear God who loveth us,
> He made and loveth all.

It is a solemn message, contrasting with the levity of the wedding feast and the sound of the loud bassoon—a message which, like that of the biblical prophet, leaves the Guest a sadder but a wiser man. At times the biblical echo is patent, as when the Albatross, like Pharaoh's host,

> . . . fell off, and sank
> Like lead into the sea.

But often it is more subtle, and part of the moral vision. As John L. Lowes' study has shown, the sources upon which Coleridge drew for this poem are manifold, but above all it was the biblical theme of divine retribution and mercy, the prophetic figure of the Mariner, and the parallelistic incremental repetition

> Alone, alone, all, all alone,
> Alone on a wide wide sea!
> And never a saint took pity on
> My soul in agony.

which endowed the poem with its supernatural fascination.

For Wordsworth, the ethical teachings of nature took on a more personal tone. The terror inspired by storms and the joy radiated by spring flowers were themselves sufficient, without the supernatural phenomena of the *Ancient Mariner*, to warn man of his moral duties. In a famous passage in the *Prelude* he relates how, when he was engaged in the boyish prank of 'borrowing' a skiff, a huge cliff seemed to rear its head and pursue him as a heaven-sent warning. It was, he realized, his guilty conscience responding to the moral impulses of nature, and from that moment he developed the germs of that philosophy whereby

> One impulse from a vernal wood
> May teach you more of man,
> Of moral evil and of good
> Than all the sages can.

Nature was no longer a tapestry of classical mythology, but had come alive with moral implications. We have already seen how, in the important preface to the *Lyrical Ballads*, he rejected poetic diction in favour of the simplicity of biblical language and imagery. But in a later preface he went much further, testifying to the greater imaginative power of Hebrew poetry and of the tradition it had inspired, and employing the term *imagination* in its new sense to denote the acme of poetic genius.

The grand storehouses of enthusiastic and meditative Imagination, of poetical as contradistinguished from human and dramatic Imagination, are the prophetic and lyrical parts of the Holy Scriptures, and the works of Milton; to which I cannot forbear to add those of Spenser. I select these writers in preference to those of ancient Greece and Rome, because the anthropomorphitism of the Pagan religion subjected the minds of the greatest poets in those countries too much to the bondage of definite form; from which the Hebrews were preserved by their abhorrence of idolatry.[1]

He tends here to over-simplify the distinction between the two literatures by the convenient tag of anthropomorphism—there seems little reason why the use of mythology in poetry should *ipso facto* produce an insistence upon form. The boot,

[1] Preface to 1815 edition.

in fact, is on the other foot; it was the Hebraic consecration of poetry to a higher spiritual purpose which made matters of purely literary form almost superfluous. Nevertheless, Wordsworth had grasped the valuable distinction between classical *form* and Hebraic *enthusiasm*, and he goes on to add that in Milton's poetry

However imbued the surface might be with classical literature, he was a Hebrew in soul; and all things tended in him towards the sublime.

In conclusion, he deduces from these instances that poetry should concentrate upon 'its worthiest objects, the external universe, the moral and religious sentiments of Man, his natural affections, and his acquired passions.' This passage leaves no doubt, therefore, that Wordsworth's own renunciation of classical mythology and his preference for a morally animated nature were prompted to no small extent by his awareness of the biblical tradition.

Nevertheless, Wordsworth's concept of the natural world was not identical with the Hebraic. As John Jones has recently argued, in the earlier poetry he was only mildly concerned with what his age called God the Great Mechanic.[1] Hence his rejection of Paley's famous simile, his refusal to

consider the Supreme Being as bearing the same relation to the Universe, as a watch-maker bears to a watch. In fact, there is nothing in the course of the religious education adopted in this country, and in the use made by us of the Holy Scriptures, that appears to me so injurious as perpetually talking about *making* by God.

He was more concerned with nature's power to communicate with man than its proof of divine creation, and it was only in his later years that he revised his earlier poems, inserting minor emendations to bring them into line with Christian belief. Yet in many of his poems, there is no need for any reservations about pantheism or Deism—the mood is captured directly from the Psalms and, throwing theological

---

[1] John Jones, *The Egotistical Sublime* (London, 1960), p. 36, referring to *Letters of William and Dorothy Wordsworth*, ed. E. de Selincourt (Oxford, 1937–9), ii, 619. The letter is dated 1814.

doubts to the winds, he has all nature bursting into a song of praise and gratitude not to a faintly camouflaged Spirit of the Universe but to the old-fashioned God of the Bible.

> Break forth into thanksgiving
> Ye banded instruments of wind and chords;
> Unite, to magnify the Ever-living,
> Your inarticulate notes with the voice of words!
> Nor hushed be service from the lowing mead,
> Nor mute the forest hum of noon;
> Thou too be heard, lone eagle! freed
> From snowy peak and cloud, attune
> Thy hungry barkings to the hymn
> Of joy, that from her utmost walls
> The six-days' work by flaming Seraphim
> Transmits to Heaven! As Deep to Deep
> Shouting through one valley calls,
> All worlds, all natures, mood and measures keep
> For praise and ceaseless gratulation, poured
> Into the ear of God, their Lord.[1]

We tend to think of Wordsworth more in terms of the gleeful dancing of daffodils than the more solemn morality of the Bible, but beneath the surface of his longer poems there often lies the world of the Scriptures. Coleridge, who was perhaps Wordsworth's most perceptive critic, remarked on one occasion that his rustic characters express sentiments and employ an elevated language unsuited to a Westmoreland farmer. Nevertheless, he adds, the characters remain credible because the reader assumes they have received an 'unambitious, but solid and religious education, which has rendered few books familiar, but the Bible, and the Liturgy, and the Hymn Book.'[2] This remark, in isolation, may seem far-fetched. Yet *Michael*, for example, has a patently biblical substructure.

The names alone—Michael and Luke—have scriptural associations, and although the work is subtitled *A Pastoral Poem*, the shepherd, we soon realize, is no Thyrsis singing disconsolately of his love, but a patriarchal figure sternly insisting on the highest moral integrity. He climbs the moun-

---

[1] *On the Power of Sound*, stanza xiii.
[2] *Biographia Literaria*, chapter xvii.

tains during storms to care for his flocks, returning each evening for his 'mess of pottage', and so exemplary a life do he and his wife lead that 'they were as a proverb in the vale/ For endless industry.' Luke is the 'son of his old age' who receives his 'hire of praise' for working with the sheep. In time, a kinsman for whom Michael had been 'bound in surety' fails, and Michael is faced with the dreadful possibility of having to sell 'a portion of his patrimonial fields'. At last it is decided that the son shall be sent to the city, but Michael's 'helpmate' realizes that, as when Benjamin is asked to part from his father Jacob, 'if thou leave thy father, he will die'. Nevertheless, the boy does receive the 'blessings of his Father's tongue' and before he departs, Michael goes through the biblical ceremony of making a heap of stones. The stones, like those of the biblical altar, are 'unhewn', and their significance is that they shall serve as a 'covenant' between them. The prodigal son becomes corrupted by the city, and the old shepherd dies heartbroken, after spending each day sitting in grief beside the unhewn stones of the covenant. What Coleridge rightly perceived, then, to be the language of the Bible rather than the dialect of the common people (except insofar as they resorted to biblical language in their daily speech) is thus more than a merely linguistic device. For the entire poem is permeated with biblical morality, with a sense of the ethically based patriarchal system and with the condemnation of city corruption as opposed to the simple dignity of guarding one's flocks and herds. The same is true of many of the longer poems. *The Norman Boy* tells of a 'dear holy shepherd' who learns of the divine reward for humble labour expressed in language strongly reminiscent of the prophetic message in the *Ancient Mariner*, coupled with hymnal rhythms.

> God of his service needeth not proud work of human skill;
> They please him best who labour most to do in peace his will:
> So let us strive to live, and to our Spirits will be given
> Such wings as when our Saviour calls, shall bear us up to heaven.

It was, in fact, the ethical quality of his work which entitled Wordsworth to feel that he was fulfilling the noblest task of the poet—that which made him the modern counterpart of the biblical prophet. Hence, in the preface to his *Excursion*, his invocation is not a conventional request for literary inspiration addressed to the classical Muse, but a prayer to the spirit of prophecy that his poetry be virtuous and of benignant influence.

> Descend, prophetic Spirit! that inspir'st
> The human Soul of universal earth,
> Dreaming on things to come: and dost possess
> A metropolitan temple in the hearts
> Of mighty Poets: upon me bestow
> A gift of genuine insight; that my Song
> With star-like virtue in its place may shine,
> Shedding benignant influence, and secure,
> Itself, from all malevolent effect
> Of those mutations that extend their sway
> Throughout the nether sphere![1]

He thought of himself as a poet-prophet of Nature, awakening mankind to those moral impulses which could soothe, purify and inspire.

If the ethical didacticism of Wordsworth's poetry was one of the distinguishing marks of its biblical indebtedness, what are we to say of Byron whose ostentatious cult of immorality would seem to place him at the opposite pole? The answer is that opposite poles attract, and that, as so often in literature (and, indeed, in life itself), there is frequently a greater kinship between diametrically opposed forces than those which are merely disparate. When a man is trying to destroy an idea, he is only too often attempting to cauterize it from his own soul. What Byron was trying to cauterize was that stern Calvinist upbringing which had left so indelible an imprint upon him. His own defiant diabolism concealed an overpowering sense of guilt, accentuated, if not totally created, by the doctrines of original sin and predestination to which he had been subjected as a child. In fact, his fundamental need for religious belief showed as a sort of uncloven hoof from beneath the hem of his scarlet robes. For all his delight in shocking the conven-

[1] Preface to the 1814 edition, 83–93.

tional piety of his contemporaries, in the intimacy of his study, he could confess:

> Frown not upon me, churlish Priest! that I
> Look not for Life where life may never be;
> I am no sneerer at thy phantasy;
> Thou pitiest me,—alas! I envy thee.[1]

It would seem to be no accident that he discarded this stanza from *Childe Harold*—it would have spoilt that public image of confident heresy he so wished to cultivate.

Nevertheless, it is necessary to distinguish between his attack on Calvinism and his very deep admiration and affection for the Old Testament itself. His drama *Cain*, for instance, is usually cited to illustrate his iconoclastic intent and, of course, on its publication it was greeted in most quarters as a piece of calculated and cynical profanity. Cain, the rationalist, challenges the unjust and capricious God, condemning him as an 'Omnipotent tyrant'. But two main points militate against accepting this stand as representing the ultimate meaning of the play. First, Byron took good care to remain scrupulously faithful to the biblical story, answering any critics in his preface with the injunction: 'Behold the Book!' Certainly the Byronic Cain is not suggested by the biblical account, but neither is it denied, and the baying of offended critics was somewhat stifled by their inability to disprove his interpretation from the biblical text itself. In fact, Byron was following the Protestant tradition of removing all exegetical encrustations in order to examine the naked text, and they had to admit the devil's right to quote Scripture.

Secondly, to regard the work in totality as deliberate heresy is to ignore not merely the ending but even the main body of the play. Lucifer, the intellectual devil, is at first a highly attractive figure. Yet Cain, by following Lucifer's persuasively reasoned arguments, is eventually led to the abhorrent crime of fratricide; and a fratricide, let us not forget, in which the innocent Abel is sympathetically presented as a suffering

---

[1] Quoted in E. W. Marjarum, *Byron as Skeptic and Believer* (Princeton, 1938), p. 30.

Christ figure. That nobly rebellious spirit of Cain's which dominates the opening of the play is, by its close, pitifully crushed. Overwhelmed by the enormity of his crime, he cries:

> And *he* who lieth there was childless! I
> Have dried the fountain of a gentle race,
> Which might have graced his recent marriage couch,
> And might have tempered this stern blood of mine,
> Uniting with our children Abel's offspring!

Mournfully he relinquishes his quest for truth, submitting to the yoke of heavenly chastisement, and Adah's prayer for Abel, 'Peace be with him!' elicits from Cain that dreadful final cry of the play: 'But with me!—' This is no justification for heresy; it is a moving projection of Byron's own spiritual dilemma, an attack not upon the Bible but on the traditional Christian interpretation of it.

In Byron's non-dramatic verse the warmth and affection he felt for the Bible is readily apparent. In his youth, he experimented with an imitation of Ossian which does, in fact, capture those rhythms of the Bible which Ossian had helped indirectly to popularize:

> Past is the race of heroes. But their fame rises on the harp; their souls ride on the wings of the wind; they hear the sound through the sighs of the storm, and rejoice in their hall of clouds.

But more significant, particularly after our discussion of his suppressed religious instinct, is an early poem in which those hymnological trends fostered by the Psalms moulded his own *Prayer of Nature*.

> Father! no prophet's laws I seek—
> *Thy* laws in Nature's works appear;—
> I own myself corrupt and weak,
> Yet will I pray, for thou wilt hear!

That helpless prostration before God and Nature which distinguishes the yearning romantic from the self-sufficient neoclassicist is the motive force in this poem, written at the age of seventeen. And lest we imagine that the hymnological source is no more than a chance resemblance in technical form, it is worth comparing another poem written at approximately the same period under classical influence in order to see how uninvolved it is; how that conscious concern with literary form pervades even the imitations of Greek and Latin poems in contrast to the intensely personal involvement typical of poems modelled on the Scriptures.

> When fierce conflicting passions urge
> The breast where love is wont to glow,
> What mind can stem the stormy surge
> Which rolls the tide of human woe?
> The hope of praise, the dread of shame,
> Can rouse the tortured breast no more;
> The wild desire, the guilty flame,
> Absorbs each wish it felt before.

This is a translation from the *Medea* of Euripides in which the subject-matter is equally concerned with passions and stormy surges. But here it is all impersonalized—passions *urge the breast* as the *Gradus* instructs them to do, whereas in the Hebraic world

> I own myself corrupt and weak,
> Yet will I pray, for thou wilt hear!

The clearest indication of his affinity to Hebraism, however, is in the collection of poems written for some *Hebrew Melodies* and published under that title in 1815. Swift remarked once in connection with his Irish birth that being born in a stable does not make one a horse, and it might be added here that writing a poem to fit a Hebrew melody does not make a poem Hebraic. Nevertheless, in this particular instance Byron consciously sought after Hebraic concepts, settings, and rhythms, delving into his own biblical readings and childhood impressions in order to recreate the world of the Scriptures—and with remarkable success.

The first of the poems, while remote from the biblical rhythms and idioms we have been examining, consciously aims at capturing from the *Song of Songs* the oriental luxuriance, the languorous yet rich passion for the dark beauty of the Shulamite.

> She walks in beauty, like the night
> Of cloudless climes and starry skies;

187

And all that's best of dark and bright
Meet in her aspect and her eyes. . . .

And on that cheek, and o'er that brow,
So soft, so calm, yet eloquent,
The smiles that win, the tints that glow,
But tell of days in goodness spent,
A mind at peace with all below,
A heart whose love is innocent.

There is a breathless hush over the whole poem, the hush of
the warm, starry Mediterranean night alluded to in the opening lines, and unlike so many of his love-poems, this one
expresses the innocence and purity of untainted love. In fact,
the only other love-poem which catches a similar mood—
There be none of Beauty's daughters—was written immediately
after the *Hebrew Melodies*, while the Hebraic, oriental mood
was still upon him.

Elsewhere, he borrows more directly from scriptural
imagery:

The wild gazelle on Judah's hills
Exulting yet may bound,
And drink from all the living rills
That gush on holy ground.

Yet the two primary themes to which he kept returning in this
collection were Saul and David on the one hand and the destruction of the Temple on the other—both themes closely
related to his own personal life and aspirations.

His identification with Saul is typical of that specifically
Protestant ability to relive within oneself the lives of Old
Testament figures; or, to put it conversely, to read the stories
of the Old Testament in terms of one's own hopes, disillusion-
ments, and fears.[1] In the melancholy Saul, soothed by the
music of David's harp, he saw an archetype of his own gloomy
temperament relieved and even enlivened by the poetry of
Psalms, and in a wider sense by the composition of his own
verse. He writes of the poetry of the 'monarch minstrel' in-
culcating virtue by its fiery power.

[1] For a fuller examination of this Protestant 'post-figuration', see my
'Shakespeare and the Biblical Stage' in the *Iowa English Yearbook* (1964).

It softened men of iron mould,
  It gave them virtues not their own;
No ear so dull, no soul so cold,
  That felt not, fired not to the tone,

and he uses the language of the Psalms to describe their
magical effect:

It made our gladden'd valleys ring,
  The cedars bow, the mountains nod.

He is infinitely more moving, however, when he projects
himself into Saul's black despair as the latter yearns for the
'wild and deep' notes which should soothe him back to peace.

My soul is dark—Oh! quickly string
  The harp I yet can brook to hear;
And let thy gentle fingers fling
  Its melting murmurs o'er mine ear. . . .
But bid the strain be wild and deep,
  Nor let thy notes of joy be first:
I tell thee, minstrel, I must weep,
  Or else this heavy heart will burst;
For it hath been by sorrow nursed,
  And ach'd in sleepless silence long;
And now 'tis doomed to know the worst,
  And break at once—or yield to song.

Where the classics, and perhaps neo-classicism even more,
provided Byron with the pivotal caesuras, the antithetical
end-stopped lines and the urbane detachment for his spark-
ingly irreverent satires, he turned to the biblical world for
those deeper passions wherewith to express his own heart-ache
and longings.

The theme of the destruction of the Temple formed, of
course, part of the contemporary surge towards national
independence, the growing sympathy for oppressed peoples of
the world which was to express itself within Byron's own life
in his identification with the Greek cause.

Tribes of the wandering foot and weary breast,
How shall ye flee away and be at rest!
The wild dove hath her nest, the fox his cave,
Mankind their country—Israel but the grave!

189

A stanza such as the above has no biblical indebtedness worthy of note, and the entire group of poems on this national theme could be ascribed to a general sociological impulse, were it not that central to this movement for national independence was a return to those cultural sources which served to unify and determine the character of each individual nation. Hence the concern with ancient English ballads, with Celtic manuscripts, and, indeed, with all primitive writings. However, for the Jewish people deprived of their homeland there was no need to ferret out forgotten manuscripts, and these poems are redolent of the Old Testament world and of its poetic techniques. In fact, his choice of the anapaestic tetrameter was a *tour de force*, since it proved to be the most effective of all English metres for capturing the undulating, pulsating rhythm of parallelism; and his vivid use of biblical imagery, his simple *and* juxtapositions create a remarkably evocative poem.

> The Assyrian came down like the wolf on the fold,
> And his cohorts were gleaming in purple and gold;
> And the sheen of their spears was like stars on the sea,
> When the blue wave rolls nightly on deep Galilee.
>
> Like the leaves of the forest when Summer is green,
> That host with their banners at sunset were seen:
> Like the leaves of the forest when Autumn hath blown,
> That host on the morrow lay wither'd and strown.

Although Browning, with all his Hebraic affinities, comes a little too late to be included in this present study, we may at least note how he employed the same anapaestic metre when he too wished to evoke the biblical scene in his *Saul*:

> Said Abner, 'At last thou art come! Ere I tell, ere thou speak,
> Kiss my cheek, wish me well!' Then I wished it and did kiss his cheek.
> And he, 'Since the King, O my friend, for thy countenance sent,
> Neither drunken nor eaten have we; nor until from his tent
> Thou return with the joyful assurance the King liveth yet,
> Shall our lip with the honey be bright, with the water be wet.'

Whether he consciously borrowed the metre from Byron it is difficult to say, but certainly the *Destruction of Sennacherib* marked the stage after Blake's prophetic books—biblical poetry, not written in a poetic prose set out as verse, but transferred to an English accentual metre which nevertheless retained the rhythmic throb of the original together with its fire and imaginative force.

> And the widows of Ashur are loud in their wail,
> And the idols are broke in the temple of Baal;
> And the might of the Gentile, unsmote by the sword,
> Hath melted like snow in the glance of the Lord!

Byron's conscious attempt to recapture the cadences and imagery of the Bible has no parallel in the writings of Shelley, in whose poetry it is virtually impossible to find a single stanza deliberately echoing the rhythms of the Scriptures; and yet of all the romantic poets none has been more consistently linked by critics with the biblical tradition. Shelley's reputation has been partially eclipsed in the present generation (not for the first time since his works were published) by the attacks of the New Critics with Dr. Leavis serving as the spearhead, and no one can deny the justice of much of their adverse criticism.[1] His poetry is frequently vague and insubstantial, he delights in charnel-houses and the less palatable aspects of the 'Gothic' school, and a vein of pseudo-Shakespeareanism runs through much of his poetic dramas. But in what may be regarded as the classic rejoinder to Leavis's attack, Frederick A. Pottle has argued that these failings are offset by some very real virtues, by virtues which still entitle Shelley to be classed among the great poets. And foremost among these virtues he cites the 'passionately religious' element in Shelley's writings whereby he looked eagerly forward to the apocalyptic era of man's spiritual redemption with 'the faith of the prophet, the faith held by the authors of Isaiah and of the Revelation', however different their concept of that redemption might be.[2]

[1] F. R. Leavis, *Revaluation* (London, 1949), pp. 203 f.

[2] Frederick A. Pottle, 'The Case of Shelley', *PMLA*, lxvii (1952), 589, reprinted in a revised from in *English Romantic Poets*, ed. M. H. Abrams (Oxford, 1960), p. 289. Bennet Weaver argues for Shelley as a biblical-type prophet in *Toward the Understanding of Shelley* (Ann Arbor, 1932).

Indeed, in much the same way as Byron's defiant diabolism did not exclude a genuine love of the Scriptures, so
Shelley's avowed atheism in no way lessened his reverence for
the beauty of biblical poetry and for the magnificent spirit
with which the prophets fought for man's social and spiritual
betterment. For all his antipathy to formal religion (or perhaps
because of it—for the biblical prophets too had condemned
the hypocrisy of a ritual emptied of spiritual content), he
read the Bible avidly, and the second Mrs. Shelley notes
repeatedly how his more general reading included 'a constant
perusal of portions of the Old Testament—the Psalms, the
Book of Job, the Prophet Isaiah, and others, the sublime
poetry of which filled him with delight'. Elsewhere she adds
that 'in English, the Bible was his constant study: he read a
great portion of it aloud in the evening'.[1]

The effect of this constant reading is to be seen primarily
in his concept of the hierophantic nature of poetry. In his
Defence of Poetry, prophecy becomes the keyword for identifying the poetic genius at its best—not in the hackneyed *vates*
equation which, since Sidney's day had been repeatedly
quoted to justify the social standing of the poet, but in a
more profound context.

Not that I assert poets to be prophets in the gross sense of the
word, or that they can foretell the form as surely as they foreknow
the spirit of events: such is the pretence of superstition, which
would make poetry an attribute of prophecy, rather than prophecy
an attribute of poetry. A poet participates in the eternal, the
infinite, and the one.

In other words, the conventional restriction of the term
prophet to *vates* or foreteller of the future, had obscured the
real identity of prophet and poet—their concern with the
eternal, unifying elements of life. 'Poetry', he informs us a
little later, 'redeems from decay the visitations of the divinity
in man', and by *divinity* he does not mean only immortality,
but that which is to form the core of his own poetry. For he
argues in this essay that the 'diviner' purpose of poetry is 'to
produce the moral improvement of man'. In fact, he is at

[1] See her notes on *The Revolt of Islam,* and on *Poems of 1817.*

pains to explain away the immoral lives of various famous poets on the grounds that the sense of beauty and love which their poetry inspired cancels out such peccadilloes; or to use the phrase from Isaiah which he himself quotes at this point, if their sins 'were as scarlet, they are now white as snow'. Again, therefore, the ethical, reforming element of romantic poetry, the belief that the poet had a more sublime function to perform than merely to amuse or instruct in the limited Augustan sense is seen to derive directly from the biblical consecration of poetry to a divine purpose.

In his preface to *Prometheus Unbound*, Shelley alluded to this distinction between the neo-classicist's desire to instruct and what he called his own 'passion for reforming the world'. Didactic poetry as such, he declared, was to him an abhorrence since it could be expressed equally effectively in prose. His own purpose was to provide the reader with

beautiful idealisms of moral excellence; aware that until the mind can love, and admire, and trust, and hope, and endure, reasoned principles of moral conduct are seeds cast away upon the highway of life which the unconscious passenger tramples into the dust, although they would bear the harvest of his happiness.

If his own poetry was not modelled on the Bible in matters of technical form, it breathed the same spirit of moral zeal, of uncompromising insistence on justice, of yearning for the messianic era. Even in the apparently classical drama which followed this preface, there lies behind the Greek myth what he once described as 'the sublime dramatic poem, *Job*', and again we are indebted to Mrs. Shelley for the information that the three themes which he chose as the groundwork for his lyrical dramas were a story of Tasso, Prometheus, and 'the *Book of Job* which he never abandoned in idea, but of which no trace remains among his papers.'[1] Perhaps the reason that he never executed the project is that *Prometheus Unbound* had already given some expression to Job's attempt to challenge the apparent injustice of the universe.

Shelley's poetic credo, the *Ode to the West Wind*, comes closest of all his poems to the biblical spirit. There we find

[1] Notes on *Prometheus Unbound*.

that same awed humility, that same prostration before the omnipotent power of nature and, not least, that same longing for spiritual union expressed by the Psalmist: 'I stretch forth my hands unto thee: my soul thirsteth after thee as a thirsty land. . . . Hear me speedily, O Lord: my spirit faileth.' In Shelley's poem, as in the Book of Job, the poet begins as a puny insignificant creature, dwarfed by the overwhelming might of creation and desperately needing the pity and mercy of heaven.

> Oh, lift me as a wave, a leaf, a cloud!
> I fall upon the thorns of life! I bleed!

But faith in the rightness of his own cause at length gives him confidence to address the Spirit almost as an equal, challenging it to use him as the instrument for a prophetic message to mankind.

> Make me thy lyre, even as the forest is:
> What if my leaves are falling like its own!
> The tumult of thy mighty harmonies
> Will take from both a deep autumnal tone,
> Sweet though in sadness.

The very symbol of the wind as inspiration is largely biblical in origin.[1] We recall the spirit of life breathed into Adam's nostrils, the divine breath revitalizing the valley of dry bones, the Voice answering Job out of the whirlwind, and Ezekiel's vision: 'Then a wind lifted me up, and I heard behind me the voice of a great rushing, "Blessed be the glory of the Lord".' In biblical Hebrew, the words *wind, spirit* and *breath* are identical (*ruach*), denoting the mysterious life-giving force which in nature blew over the face of the waters at the Creation, and in man inspire prophetic vision. In Shelley's *Ode*, the wind performs precisely this dual function, symbolizing on the one hand the resurrective forces of nature quickening a new birth out of the dead matter of the universe, and on the other hand, the Spirit of Prophecy awakening in

[1] See M. H. Abrams 'The Correspondent Breeze: a Romantic Metaphor', reprinted in a revised form from the *Kenyon Review*, xix (1957), 113, in his *English Romantic Poets*, ed. cit., p. 37.

the poet the apocalyptic vision of a messianic springtime for mankind:

> Be thou, Spirit fierce,
> My spirit! Be thou me, impetuous one! . . .
> Be through my lips to unwakened earth
>
> The trumpet of a prophecy! O, Wind,
> If Winter comes, can Spring be far behind?

For the romantic poet, the biblical ethos had been partially secularized. God had been largely replaced by the Spirit of Nature, the brotherhood of man by the pantisocratic society, and the messiah by the dawn of the New World. Yet for all that, there remained a strong spiritual kinship with the world of the Old Testament, not only in the emotional rhythms and vivid images which parallelism had helped to foster, but also in this vibrant declaration of faith—the conviction that poetry at its best should be the *trumpet of a prophecy*, awakening the sleeping souls of mankind to the beauties of Creation in a moral universe.

Bibliography

Abrams, M. H. *The Mirror and the Lamp* (New York, 1958).
Ainsworth, E. G., and Noyes, C. E. *Christopher Smart* (Columbia, 1943).
Auerbach, E. *Mimesis* (New York, 1957).
Baroway, I. 'The Accentual Theory of Hebrew Prosody', *ELH*, xvii (1950), 155.
— 'The Bible in the Renaissance', *JEGP*, xxxii (1933), 478.
— 'The Hebrew Hexameter', *ELH*, ii (1935), 66.
— 'The Imagery of Spenser and the *Song of Songs*', *JEGP*, xxxiii (1934), 23.
— 'The Lyre of David', *ELH*, viii (1941), 119.
Bate, W. J. *From Classic to Romantic* (Cambridge, Massachusetts, 1946).
Beer, J. B. *Coleridge the Visionary* (London, 1959).
Binyon, R. L. *The Case of Christopher Smart* (London, 1934).
Bishop, M. *Blake's Hayley* (London, 1951).
Bond, D. F. ' "Distrust" of Imagination in English Neo-Classicism', *PQ*, xiv (1935), 54.
Bond, W. H. *Jubilate Agno* (London, 1954).
Bosker, A. *Literary Criticism in the Age of Johnson* (Gröningen, 1930).
Bradner, L. 'The Latin Drama of the Renaissance', *Studies in the Renaissance*, iv (1957).
Broadus, E. K. 'Addison's Influence on the Development of Interest in Folk Poetry in the Eighteenth Century', *MP*, viii (1910), 123.
Bronowski, J. *William Blake: A man without a mask* (London, 1944).
Brooke, S. A. *Naturalism in English Poetry* (London, 1920).
Brown, P. H. *Life of Goethe* (London, 1920).
Cecil, Lord David. *The Stricken Deer* (London, 1929).
Chew, S. C. *The Crescent and the Rose* (New York, 1937).
Clark, A. F. B. *Boileau and the French Classical Criticism in England* (Paris, 1925).

Conant, M. P. *The Oriental Tale in England in the Eighteenth Century* (New York, 1908).

Cowl, R. P. *The Theory of Poetry in England* (Oxford, 1913).

Crane, R. S. 'An Early Eighteenth-Century Enthusiast for Primitive Poetry: John Husbands', *MLN*, xxxvii (1922), 27.

Creed J. M. and Smith, J. S. B. (eds.). *Religious Thought in the Eighteenth Century* (Cambridge, 1934).

Crofts, J. E. V. *Eighteenth-Century Literature: an Oxford Miscellany* (Oxford, 1909).

Damon, S. F. *William Blake: his philosophy and symbols* (Gloucester, Mass., 1958).

Doughty, O. *The English Lyric in the Age of Reason* (London, 1922).

— *Forgotten Lyrics of the Eighteenth Century* (London, 1924).

Draper, J. W. *Eighteenth-century English Aesthetics: a bibliography* (Heidelberg, 1931).

— *The Theory of Translation in the Eighteenth Century* (Hague, 1921).

Durham, W. H. ed. *Critical Essays of the Eighteenth Century* (London, 1915).

Edwards, T. R. *This Dark Estate: a reading of Pope* (Berkeley, 1963).

Fairchild, H. N. *The Noble Savage* (New York, 1928).

— *Religious Trends in English Poetry*, 4 vols. (New York, 1939–57).

Fitzgerald, M. M. *First Follow Nature: Primitivism in English Poetry 1725–1750* (New York, 1947).

Fisch, H. 'The Analogy of Nature', *JTS*, vi (1955), 161.

Foerster, D. M. *Homer in English Criticism* (New Haven, 1947).

Freimarck, V. *The Bible in Eighteenth Century English Criticism* (1950). An unpublished thesis at Cornell University Library.

— 'The Bible and Neo-classical Views of Style', *JEGP*, li (1952), 507.

Frye, N. *Fearful Symmetry* (Princeton, 1958).

Gallaway, F. *Reason, Rule and Revolt in English Classicism* (New York, 1940).

Gardner, H. *The Limits of Literary Criticism* (Oxford, 1956).

Goad, C. M. *Horace in the English Literature of the Eighteenth Century* (New Haven, 1918).

Gosse, E. *Two Pioneers of Romanticism* (London, 1915).

Gray, G. B. *The Forms of Hebrew Poetry* (London, 1915).

Hartley, L. 'The Worm and the Thorn: a study of Cowper's *Olney Hymns*', *JR*, xxix (1949), 220.

Havens, R. D. *The Influence of Milton on English Poetry* (Cambridge, Mass., 1922).

— 'Poetic Diction of the English Classicists' in *Anniversary Papers Presented to G. L. Kittredge* ((Boston/London, 1913).

— 'Romantic Aspects of the Age of Pope', *PMLA*, xxvii (1912), 297.
— 'The Structure of Smart's *Song to David*', *RES*, xiv (1938), 178.
Henn, T. R. *Longinus and English Criticism* (Cambridge, 1934).
Highet, G. *The Classical Tradition* (Oxford, 1949).
Hipple, W. J. *The Beautiful, the Sublime, and the Picturesque* (Carbondale, 1957).
Hooker, E. N. 'The Discussion of Taste from 1750 to 1770', *PMLA*, xlix (1934), 577.
Horning, M. E. *Evidences of the Romantic Treatment of Religious Elements in Late Eighteenth Century Minor Poetry* (Washington, 1932).
Hustvedt, S. B. *Ballad Criticism in Scandinavia and Great Britain During the Eighteenth Century* (New York, 1916).
Jack, I. *Augustan Satire* (Oxford, 1957).
Johnson, J. W. 'The Meaning of *Augustan*', *JHI*, xix (1958).
Jones, John. *The Egotistical Sublime* (London, 1960).
Knight, D. *Pope and the Heroic Tradition* (New Haven, 1951).
Laing, M. *The Poems of Ossian* (Edinburgh, 1805).
Lewisohn, L. *Goethe* (New York, 1949).
Lovejoy, A. O. *The Great Chain of Being* (Cambridge, Mass., 1936).
— *Essays in the History of Ideas* (Baltimore, 1948).
Lovejoy, A. O. and Boas, G. *Primitive and Related Ideas in Antiquity* (Baltimore, 1935).
Lowth, R. *Isaiah: a new translation* (London, 1774).
— *The Sacred Poetry of the Hebrews* tr. G. Gregory (London, 1835).
Martin, L. C. 'Henry Vaughan and the Theme of Infancy' in *Seventeenth Century Studies Presented to Sir Herbert Grierson* (Oxford, 1938).
McCutcheon, R. P. 'Another Burlesque of Addison's Ballad Criticism', *SP*, xxiii (1926), 451.
Monk, S. H. *The Sublime* (New York, 1935).
— 'A Grace Beyond the Reach of Art'. *JHI*, v (1944), 131.
Moore, C. A. 'The Return to Nature in English Poetry of the Eighteenth Century', *SP*, xiv (1917).
Moulton, R. G. *The Modern Reader's Bible* (New York, 1907).
Murray, G. *The Classical Tradition in Poetry* (Oxford, 1927).
Neff, E. *The Poetry of History* (New York, 1947).
Nicolson, M. H. *Mountain Gloom and Mountain Glory* (Ithaca, New York, 1959).
— *Newton Demands the Muse* (Princeton, 1946).
Nitchie, E. *Vergil and the English Poets* (Columbia, 1919).
Osborne, E. *Oriental Diction and Theme in English Verse, 1740–1840* (Lawrence, 1916).

Pinto, V. de Sola. 'Isaac Watts and William Blake', *RES*, xx (1944), 214.

— 'Isaac Watts and the Adventurous Muse', *ES*, xx (1934), 86.

Pottle, F. A. 'The Case of Shelley', *PMLA*, lxvii (1952), 589.

Quayle, T. *Poetic Diction* (London, 1924).

Quinlan, M. J. 'Cowper's Imagery', *JEGP*, xlvii (1948), 276.

Reynolds, M. *The Treatment of Nature in English Poetry* (Chicago, 1896).

Saintsbury, G. *A History of Criticism* (Edinburgh/London, 1917).

Sarma, D. S. 'Two Minor Critics of the Age of Pope', *MLR*, xiv (1919), 386.

Schmitz, R. M. *Hugh Blair* (New York, 1948).

Schwarz, W *Principles and Problems of Biblical Translation* (Cambridge, 1955).

Shairp, J. C. *On the Interpretation of Nature* (Edinburgh, 1877).

Simmons, B. *Some Aspects of the Treatment of the Psalms and the Song of Solomon in English Eighteenth Century Literature* (1937). An unpublished thesis at London University Library.

Smalley, B. *The Study of the Bible in the Middle Ages* (Oxford, 1952).

Smith, L. P. *Four Words: Romantic, Originality, Creative, Genius* (Oxford, 1924).

Spingarn, J. E. *Critical Essays of the Seventeenth Century* (Oxford, 1908–9).

Stead, W. F. *Rejoice in the Lamb* (London, 1939).

Sutherland, J. *A Preface to Eighteenth-Century Poetry* (Oxford, 1950).

Thomson, J. A. K. *The Classical Background of English Literature* (London, 1948).

Tillotson, G. 'Eighteenth-Century Poetic Diction', *ES*, xxv (1939), 59.

— *On the Poetry of Pope* (Oxford, 1938).

Tinker, C. B. *Nature's Simple Plan* (Princeton, 1922).

Van Tieghem, P. *Le Préromantisme* (Paris, 1924).

— *Ossian en France* (Paris, 1917).

Vines, W. S. *The Course of English Classicism* (London, 1930).

Wassermann, E. R. *The Subtler Language* (Baltimore, 1959).

Watson, F. *The English Grammar Schools to 1660* (Cambridge, 1908).

Weaver, B. *Toward the Understanding of Shelley* (Ann Arbor, 1932).

Wellek, R. *The Rise of English Literary History* (Chapel Hill, 1941).

Wells, E. K. *The Ballad Tree* (London, 1950).

Whitney, L. *Primitivism and the Idea of Progress* (Baltimore, 1934).

Willey, B. *The Eighteenth Century Background* (London, 1950).

Williams, A. 'The Two Matters: Classical and Christian in the Renaissance', *SP*, xxxviii (1941), 158.

Williamson, G. 'The Restoration Revolt Against Enthusiasm', *SP*, xxx, (1933) 571.

Wood, P. S. 'The Opposition to Neo-Classicism in England between 1660 and 1700', *PMLA*, xliii (1928), 182.

Index